Southern
Snacks

Southern Snacks

77 RECIPES FOR SMALL BITES WITH BIG FLAVORS

Perre Coleman Magness

PHOTOGRAPHS BY Justin Fox Burks

The University of North Carolina Press   Chapel Hill

The University of North Carolina Press has been a
member of the Green Press Initiative since 2003.

Cover photograph by Justin Fox Burks

Library of Congress Cataloging-in-Publication Data
Names: Magness, Perre, 1940– author. |
    Burks, Justin Fox, photographer.
Title: Southern snacks : 77 recipes for small bites
    with big flavors / Perre Coleman Magness ;
    photographs by Justin Fox Burks.
Description: Chapel Hill : The University of
    North Carolina Press, [2018] | Includes index.
Identifiers: LCCN 2018001365| ISBN 9781469636726
    (cloth : alk. paper) | ISBN 9781469636696 (ebook)
Subjects: LCSH: Cooking, American—Southern style. |
    Snack foods—Southern States.
Classification: LCC TX715.2.S68 M316 2018 |
    DDC 641.5975—dc23 LC record available at
    https://lccn.loc.gov/2018001365

Contents

Southern Snacks

You don't need a silver fork to eat good food.

—PAUL PRUDHOMME

It is no great secret that southerners love to eat. Or that huge parts of our lives revolve around food. The need to feed is born into us. We bring food to new parents and the recently bereaved, and no family gathering would be complete without some nostalgic family dishes prepared the way grandma used to make it. The most iconic images of southern food are often the groaning boards laden with bowls and skillets and platters of abundance: piles of fried chicken, greens, field peas, mayonnaise salads, gelatin molds, casseroles, baskets of biscuits and cornbread, cakes, pies, and cookies. Southerners adore a generous Sunday dinner surrounded by good people and good food, dinner being the big midday meal while supper is the evening one. The use of southern ingredients are just as evident in our snacks as in our suppers, from the shrimp of the coastal states to the crawfish of the bayou, the country ham of the mountains, and the catfish of the Delta. We delight in okra and field peas, sweet potatoes and buttermilk, all in small-plate form.

But southerners are just as creative and generous with the simple snack. I would argue that there is no food southerners excel at more than the small bite. We often call it pick-up food. Food for tailgating or watching the game on TV. Food for baby showers and sip and sees. Derby-watching days or cocktail parties. Holiday buffets and funeral spreads. Garden clubs, book clubs, Bible study, and bridge parties. We love a full spread of little bites—lots of choice and, well, lots. Dips and spreads and little filled biscuits, cheese molds and cheese coins, pickled vegetables and crispy little pieces of fried. Even at a party with a buffet overflowing with delicious supper dishes, there will be little silver bowls of seasoned nuts, or plates of cheese straws scattered about the house. And chefs in the South have caught on. From the finest restaurants to pop-up projects and food trucks, chefs in the South are offering little bites and lots of variety. And it stands to reason. When southerners congregate to celebrate and bloviate we like lots of choices, small bites that keep us mobile, mixing, and mingling. Loquacious southerners like to work a room, to find out about your mama and them and what you think of the team's chances next year. The standard practice for the big southern wedding is a buffet reception rather than a seated dinner, so guests can catch up with as many friends old and new as possible, and then get out on that dance floor. We often show our love through cooking food, and that motivates the southerner to get into the kitchen instead of the plastic-tub aisle at the grocery. Why buy machine-made hummus when you can use our beautiful, local field peas to take it up a notch?

Generations of southerners know that it is just not right to have someone in your home and not offer them a little bite of something. It is wise always to have some cheese straws in the freezer or a block of cream cheese and a jar of pepper jelly on hand. But small bites aren't just company food. Southerners feel comforted knowing that there is a bowl of pimento cheese in the refrigerator to snack on. Or a jar of comeback sauce for dipping anything from vegetables to saltines. It is reassuring to know that there is an old fruitcake tin full of seasoned nuts on the counter or some country ham on hand to fill our bellies. And in the South, we love a culinary project, from a pig pickin' to an oyster roast, a fish fry or a crawfish boil—food for your fingers and hands, the kind everyone hovers over, hoping no one notices exactly how much they've eaten.

Southerners have perfected the art of snacking, and now it's time to share our expertise with the rest of the world.

Dips and Spreads

Mississippi Sin

I can't even begin to imagine how this dip got its name, other than that it is cheesy and rich and a little spicy. I have also seen it named Savannah sin and southern sin, but I am not wading into that debate. The most traditional way to serve this dip is baked in a hollowed-out bread loaf, but it can be heated and served in a baking dish. It is also good cold.

SERVES A CROWD

Beat the grated cheese, cream cheese, and sour cream in the bowl of a stand mixer until well combined. Add the chopped ham, green chiles, and green onions, then the Worcestershire, hot sauce, pepper, and salt, and beat until well blended. At this point, the dip can be covered and refrigerated for 24 hours.

When ready to serve, preheat the oven to 350°.

Cut a thin slice from the top of the bread loaf and gently hollow out the center, leaving a thick wall of bread around the cavity. Reserve the bread pieces. Fill the hollowed bread loaf with the dip and replace the top. Wrap the dip-filled loaf with foil and place on a baking sheet. Bake for 1 hour, until the dip is gooey and melty. Unwrap the loaf and transfer to a serving platter.

Serve with crackers, corn chips, or toasted bread cubes.

8 ounces sharp cheddar cheese, grated

8 ounces cream cheese, softened

1½ cups sour cream

½ cup chopped cooked ham (from about 3 ounces)

1 (4-ounce) can chopped green chiles, undrained

3 green onions, white and some dark green parts, finely chopped

1 teaspoon Worcestershire sauce

½ teaspoon hot sauce (such as Crystal)

½ teaspoon freshly ground black pepper

Kosher salt to taste

1 round loaf French bread

Creamy Collard Dip,
Pimento Cheese–Style

5 strips of bacon, chopped

1 small yellow onion,
   finely diced

¼ cup water

1 (4-ounce) jar diced
   pimentos, rinsed and
   drained

1 clove garlic, finely minced

1 (16-ounce) bag frozen
   chopped collard greens,
   thawed and well drained

8 ounces cream cheese,
   softened

4 ounces sharp cheddar
   cheese, grated

½ cup sour cream

¼ cup mayonnaise,
   preferably Duke's

Kosher salt and freshly
   ground black pepper
   to taste

Hot sauce (such as Crystal),
   to taste (optional)

Hot spinach dip was all the rage during my youth, served warm with lots of cheese. But I think we can go more southern than that by combining collard greens with the fabulous flavor of pimento cheese. You still get warm and melty and gooey, but with a twist.

SERVES 10–12

Cook the bacon in a large skillet until crispy and remove to paper towels with a slotted spoon to drain. Pour the bacon grease into a measuring cup and let cool briefly. Add 2 tablespoons of grease back to the skillet. Cook the onions over medium-high heat until they are soft and translucent and just beginning to brown, then add the water and cook until it has evaporated and the onions are a light toffee color, stirring frequently. Add the pimentos and stir. Cook for about 3 minutes, then add the garlic and cook for a further minute. Stir in the collard greens, separating them and distributing the onions and pimentos evenly. Cook until the collards are heated through and soft. Add the cream cheese, cut into cubes, and stir until melted. Add the grated cheddar and stir until melted. Stir in the sour cream and mayonnaise until the dip is smooth and creamy. Add the crumbled bacon and stir until all the ingredients are well distributed. Scrape the dip into a 2-quart baking dish.

The dip can be cooled, covered, and refrigerated at this point for up to a day.

Preheat the oven to 350°. Bake the dip until it is warm through and bubbling, about 15 minutes. Serve immediately with corn chips or toasted baguette pieces.

RO-TEL

The most iconic southern snack, the one I have probably eaten more often, in more places, and for more occasions than any other, is, frankly, Ro-Tel. Ro-Tel is the brand name for canned diced tomatoes and green chiles, and when mixed with a block of melted Velveeta, it is truly the ultimate cheese dip. Though you very occasionally see recipes in cookbooks for Ro-Tel Dip, it is universally called simply Ro-Tel. As in, "I'll bring Ro-Tel," or "Let's make some Ro-Tel." I don't know if some enterprising home chef invented Ro-Tel or if it originally came from the label on the can or the box of Velveeta, but for many years it was printed on both.

Ro-Tel is for watching the game at home or to take tailgating. People make it for holiday parties, office parties, teenage gatherings, book clubs, and girls' nights. Men who can't cook, or won't admit to it, often say the only thing they know how to make is Ro-Tel.

Ro-Tel is sometimes made on the stove, now more often made in the microwave, and some people keep it in a slow cooker so it stays warm. Ro-Tel must be served hot or it is just a gooey mess.

For devotees of Ro-Tel, there is a dish in their collection that becomes known as the Ro-Tel dish, because that is what it is most often used for—a round Pyrex casserole is popular. For many years, mine was a white ceramic soufflé dish with sunflowers that was a college graduation gift to help stock my first apartment. Years of use and countless batches of Ro-Tel at parties of varying intensity and the dish chipped, cracked, and finally broke. I have not yet found a suitable replacement.

Texas Crabgrass

I found this recipe in a compilation of community cookbooks when I owned my first small home. I made it for parties all the time: the expensive and rare (at the time) crabmeat seemed impossibly chic and gourmet. Sometimes I served it in a sterling silver chafing dish borrowed from a friend who'd inherited it from her great-grandmother. I felt like a real grown-up serving this dish with uniformly browned toast points or delicate pastry shells. Truth is, it's just as good with corn chips.

SERVES 12–14

Cook the spinach according to the package instructions. Drain in a colander, pressing out as much liquid as you can.

Melt the butter in a large, deep skillet over medium-high heat. Sauté the onions until soft and translucent, but do not let them brown. Add the garlic and sauté for a further minute. Remove from the heat and stir in the Marsala, nutmeg, and cooked spinach. Add the crabmeat and use a fork to combine everything well. A fork helps to break up the crab and evenly distribute the spinach. Add the Parmesan and the cream, and stir to combine. Season to taste with hot sauce, salt, and pepper.

Scoop the spread into a casserole dish. The dish can be made up to a day ahead, covered, and refrigerated at this point. When ready to serve, reheat the spread in a 350° oven until hot and bubbly. Serve immediately or transfer to a chafing dish. Serve with hearty crackers or baguette slices, or little phyllo pastry cups for filling.

1 (12-ounce) package frozen chopped spinach
¼ cup (½ stick) unsalted butter
1 medium white onion, finely diced
2 cloves garlic, minced
¼ cup Marsala wine
½ teaspoon ground nutmeg
8 ounces pasteurized lump crabmeat
¾ cup grated Parmesan cheese
2 tablespoons heavy cream
Dash or 2 of hot sauce (such as Crystal)
Kosher salt and freshly ground black pepper to taste

Sweet Potato and Roasted Garlic Dip

1 large or 2 medium
    sweet potatoes
    (to equal 14 ounces)
25 peeled garlic cloves
1 teaspoon olive oil
4–5 fresh sage leaves
1 tablespoon sorghum syrup
1 teaspoon kosher salt
½ teaspoon sweet paprika
½ teaspoon freshly ground
    black pepper
Pinch of cayenne pepper
12 ounces plain Greek
    whole milk yogurt

This dip is complex in its simplicity. The natural notes of the ingredients—sweet, earthy potatoes and rich roasted garlic—marry perfectly. Grassy sorghum and woodsy sage add edge and interest.

MAKES ABOUT 2 CUPS

Preheat the oven to 350°. Wash the sweet potato well, and while it is still damp, wrap it tightly in aluminum foil. Place it on a rack in the oven. Place the garlic on another piece of aluminum foil and toss with the olive oil. Wrap the garlic tightly in a little hobo pack and place it on the rack in the oven as well. Bake for 50–60 minutes, until the potato is soft and the garlic is golden brown and soft. Check every 20 minutes, because one might finish before the other.

When the potato is cool enough to handle, peel it. Start with a swivel peeler, but you will probably be able to pull most of the skin off with your fingers. Place the soft flesh in the bowl of a food processor fitted with the metal blade. Add the roasted garlic and leave until completely cool.

Roughly tear the sage leaves and add them to the potatoes and garlic. Add the sorghum, salt, paprika, pepper, and cayenne and blend until smooth. Add the yogurt and blend until smooth and dippable.

Refrigerate for several hours to allow the flavors to blend. Serve with pita chips.

Carolina Caviar

Take simple, staple ingredients from the southern kitchen—black-eyed peas and corn—and turn them into a festive party dish. That's true southern ingenuity and why I assume this dish is called caviar. I have seen versions listed as Texas caviar and by the outmoded name Dixie caviar. This dip is another community cookbook staple, but the classic version is usually made with bottled Italian dressing. I've switched that out for bacon vinaigrette to punch up the southern flavor. Carolina Caviar is a popular, hearty tailgating snack and the perfect party dip for New Year's Day, when eating black-eyed peas is said to bring good luck.

SERVES A BIG CROWD

For the dip, place the black-eyed peas in a pot and cover with water by about 1 inch. Bring to a boil, skim off any foam that rises, and reduce the heat to low. Simmer the peas for about 20 minutes, until they are tender but still have a little bite. Drain and rinse the peas in a large colander and leave them to cool.

While the peas are cooking, finely dice the tomatoes, onions, and peppers. You want a small dice so that the dip can be easily scooped up with chips.

When the peas are cooled, add the corn and the chopped vegetables to the colander. Add the chopped parsley and stir to combine. Scoop everything into a large, sturdy zip-top bag. Seal the bag and toss it around to distribute all the ingredients evenly.

For the bacon vinaigrette, place the bacon grease, oil, vinegar, sorghum, hot sauce, and pepper in the carafe of a blender and blend until smooth and creamy. Taste and add salt if you like.

Pour the vinaigrette over the dip in the bag, seal, and toss to coat all the vegetables. Place the bag on a plate in case of spills and refrigerate for at least 12 hours, but up to 2 days is fine. You want the flavors to meld and mellow. Shake the bag around every so often.

Before serving, place a colander over a bowl and drain the dip. If you feel it needs it, you can stir a little bit of the dressing back into the dip, but you don't want it too oily and drippy, or it will

FOR THE DIP
2 (12-ounce) bags frozen
    black-eyed peas
1 (12-ounce) bag frozen
    yellow corn kernels,
    thawed and drained
2 plum tomatoes
1 small yellow onion
1 green bell pepper
1 red bell pepper
1 jalapeño pepper
    (2 if you are like that)
¼ cup finely chopped
    parsley

FOR THE BACON VINAIGRETTE
¼ cup bacon drippings,
    not solidified (see Note)
½ cup vegetable oil
¼ cup apple cider vinegar
1 tablespoon sorghum syrup
    or dark honey
1 teaspoon hot sauce (such
    as Crystal), to taste
Generous grinding of black
    pepper
Kosher salt (optional)

make the chips soggy and the whole affair difficult to eat. You can stir in a bit of salt if you think it needs it.

Serve with big scooping corn chips.

Note: If you'd like, you can cook about 5 strips of bacon, use the grease for the vinaigrette and stir the chopped crispy bacon into the dip.

TAILGATING

There are certain activities that anyone in any particular town, city, state, or region is expected to have participated in. Wouldn't you be surprised by someone living in Hawaii who had never been to the beach? Or shocked by a resident of Paris who had never seen the Eiffel Tower?

Well, I have one of those surprising confessions. I have never been to an SEC football game. You would not believe the looks of shock and horror that cross the faces of people who hear this tragic tale. I have only in fact been to one college football game, and that was freshman year at my small school in Connecticut, and to be honest, that's not really the same thing. It's not that I have an issue or a problem with big-time college football: the opportunity has just never presented itself (and yes, I will be expecting some invitations after writing this). But I've lived in the South long enough to have a full understanding of the spirit of tailgating. Whether it is setting up chandeliered tents in the Grove at Ole Miss, sailing with the Vol Navy in Knoxville, prepping the grill at Tiger Lane in Memphis, or boulevarding at SMU, traditions run strong— and the food is as important as the game.

TAILGATING RECIPES

Mississippi Sin

Texas Crabgrass

Deviled Egg Spread

Cheddar and Pepper Jelly Crumble Bars

Country Ham Cheesecake

Citrus Pickled Shrimp

Smoked Catfish Spread

Bama Wings with White Sauce

Sweet and Spicy Pecan Pepper

Cocktail Bacon

Barbecue Rillettes

Overnight Onions

Nuts and Bolts

Smoky Butter Bean Spread

10 ounces fresh butter
　　beans (or thawed frozen)
1 small smoked ham hock
　　(about 5 ounces), or
　　5 ounces smoked bacon
4 cloves garlic, peeled
2 bay leaves
¼ cup (½ stick) unsalted
　　butter, room temperature
1 tablespoon chopped
　　parsley
Kosher salt and freshly
　　ground black pepper

I don't know what the regional or botanical difference is, or if there is any, but I have always called the little, flat kidney-shaped green beans frequently called lima beans, "butter beans." Maybe because everything sounds better with butter.

MAKES ABOUT 1 ½ CUP

Put the butter beans, ham hock, garlic, and bay leaves in a pot and cover with water by about 2 inches. Bring to a boil and skim off any foam that rises, then lower the heat, cover the pot, and cook for 2 hours, until the beans are very tender.

Place a colander over a bowl and drain the beans, reserving the cooking liquid. Remove the ham hock and the bay leaves, but keep the garlic with the beans. Leave the beans and the strained liquid to cool.

When the butter beans are cool, put them in a food processor with the butter and parsley. Add a generous pinch of salt and generous grinds of black pepper and process until the beans break down. Drizzle in some cooking liquid, a tablespoon at a time, until you have a spreadable paste. Some chunky pieces of butter bean are fine, but you want to have a spreadable consistency. Season well with salt and pepper, and stir to blend.

Scrape the spread into a bowl, cover, and refrigerate for a few hours to allow the flavors to combine. The spread will keep, covered in the fridge, up to 2 days. Serve with hearty crackers or baguette slices.

If you'd like, you can shred the meat from the ham hock and use it to top the spread.

Field Pea Hummus

8 ounces purple hull
   field peas
2 tablespoons fresh
   lemon juice
1 teaspoon chopped
   fresh thyme
1 teaspoon kosher salt
1 clove garlic, finely minced
6 tablespoons olive oil

I had a wonderful, silky field pea hummus at Miller Union Restaurant in Atlanta. As is sometimes the case, I rather assumed that it was some secret chef preparation a mere mortal could never achieve. But I ran into Chef Steven Satterfield at the Southern Foodways Alliance Symposium and raved about his hummus. He casually said, "Oh, it's easy. Blanch the peas and blend them with some lemon and thyme." So I set to work on my own version, and although I do think there is a little magic cheffy secret to his recipe, mine is pretty darn good.

MAKES ABOUT ¾ CUP

Place the purple hulls in a large bowl and cover with water. Let the peas settle, then remove any floaters and pick out any fragments or bad peas. Use a slotted spoon to remove the peas to a large pot, leaving behind any debris.

Add water to the pot to just cover the peas. Bring to a boil, then skim off any scum or foam that rises to the top. Lower the heat to medium and cook for 20 minutes, until the peas are tender with a little bite to them, then drain and immediately them plunge into a bowl of ice water to stop the cooking. When the peas are completely cold, drain thoroughly and transfer to the bowl of a food processor.

Add the lemon juice, thyme, salt, and garlic and process until you have a smooth, thick paste, scraping down the sides of the bowl occasionally. With the motor running, drizzle in the oil, stopping a couple of times to scrape down the sides of the bowl. Process for 3–5 minutes, until you have a fine, smooth paste.

Scrape the hummus into a wire sieve set over a bowl. Using a sturdy spatula or wooden spoon, press the hummus through the sieve. Scrape the pressed hummus from bottom of the sieve with a clean spatula into the bowl several times. Press as much of the paste through the sieve as possible; you want only a few very

dry tablespoons of paste leftover in the sieve. This will create a smoother texture and a brighter color.

Whisk the pressed hummus well to combine and scrape into a serving bowl. Cover and refrigerate a few hours to allow the flavors to blend. Bring to room temperature before serving, drizzled with a little olive oil if you like.

Hot Vidalia Onion Soufflé

I think this dip has been served at almost every party I have ever been to in Memphis. In fact, sometimes when divvying up the what-to-bring assignments, the question is, "Who's bringing the onion soufflé?" It appears in the ubiquitous Junior League of Memphis cookbook *Heart and Soul*, and it's quick, easy to make, and will be devoured by anyone who comes face-to-face with it. That recipe calls for frozen onions, but I prefer to use the South's own sweet Vidalia onions. My version makes a lot of dip, but I have never seen a dish that wasn't scraped clean at the end of a party. Fritos Scoops seem to be the favorite dipper, but you can also serve it more elegantly with little toasts for spreading.

2 medium Vidalia onions, about 1½ pounds

24 ounces cream cheese, room temperature

½ cup mayonnaise, preferably Duke's

8 ounces Swiss cheese, grated

SERVES A BIG CROWD

Peel the onions and dice them finely. I like a very small dice so that it's easy to pick up the dip with chips.

Beat the cream cheese and mayonnaise together in the bowl of a stand mixer until smooth. Add the onions and the grated Swiss and beat until everything is well combined. Scrape down the sides of the bowl a couple of times during mixing. Scrape the dip into a 9 × 13-inch baking dish.

At this point, you can cover the dip and refrigerate for up to a day. When ready to bake, preheat the oven to 350°. Bake the dip uncovered for about 15 minutes, until hot through and bubbling. Serve with corn chips.

Benedictine

The story goes that Louisville caterer Jennie Benedict created this cool cucumber spread and served it in the tearoom she opened in 1911. It became an iconic dish in Louisville and other parts of Kentucky but hasn't radiated much out of the state. Which is a shame, because it is simple, cool, and refreshing, and everyone in the hot and humid South should want it all the time. Benedictine is perfect on dainty tea sandwiches or as a dip for crudités. A few drops of green food coloring is traditional, so I include it, and it does distinguish the spread as cucumber-based, but it's up to you. Of course, this classic Kentucky dish is perfect for a Derby Day party.

1 seedless cucumber (about 12 ounces), peeled
¼ small yellow onion (about 1½ ounces)
8 ounces cream cheese, softened
½ teaspoon kosher salt
¼ teaspoon white pepper
2 dashes hot sauce (such as Crystal)
2–3 drops green food coloring

MAKES 1½ CUPS

Grate the cucumber and the onion together with the grating blade of a food processor. Scrape the grated vegetables into a strainer set over a bowl. Let sit to drain for about an hour, then transfer the mix to a tea towel. Squeeze out as much liquid as possible, then put the mix back into the food processor, now fitted with the steel blade. It's important to remove as much liquid as possible from the cucumbers, or you will end up with a watery mess.

Add the cream cheese, salt, pepper, and hot sauce and process until smooth. Add the food coloring a drop at time to create a cucumbery green tint.

Scoop the benedictine into a bowl, cover, and refrigerate until ready to use. The benedictine will keep, covered in the fridge, for 3 days.

Bourbon-Spiked Caramelized Onion and Bacon Dip

8 strips of bacon
2 medium yellow onions, finely diced (about 4 cups)
1 teaspoon kosher salt
¼ cup plus 1 tablespoon bourbon, divided
1 tablespoon light brown sugar
8 ounces cream cheese, softened
1 cup mayonnaise, preferably Duke's
1 cup sour cream
Generous grinds of black pepper

I have been making a version of caramelized onion dip for ages. I take it to parties, lake weekends, family gatherings, and football-watching events. I get requests for it, and it is always absolutely vacuumed up. But when you are an avid cook, you constantly want to challenge yourself. So after years of making this dish, I set out to rev it up a bit, change things. And now that I've hit on this recipe, I'm not sure why I didn't think of it ages ago. It combines some of my favorite flavors—sweet caramelized onions, smoky bacon, and bourbon—with amazing results. This dip is decadent; it is unquestionably rich. But it will blow those you serve it to away. The bourbon adds this little zip and edge of sweetness. It is delicious hot and bubbly but also pretty darn good cold (that's how I serve my regular onion dip). It's great spread on crackers or served with big corn chips.

SERVES 10–12

Cook the bacon strips in a large skillet until crispy. Remove them with a slotted spoon to a plate lined with paper towels. Leave the bacon grease to cool, then pour it into a bowl or jar. Wipe out the skillet to remove any browned or burned bits. If you cook the onions in the sizzling-hot grease, they are likely to burn.

Pour 2 tablespoons of bacon grease back in the skillet and return it to medium heat. Add the onions and salt and stir well to coat. Cook until the onions are soft and glassy, about 10 minutes, stirring frequently. Keep the heat at medium to prevent the onions from scorching. When the onions begin to turn a light toffee color, add ¼ cup of the bourbon and the brown sugar, stir well, and cover the pan. Continue to cook over medium heat, stirring frequently, until the onions are amber brown, the color of that good bourbon. If at any point the onions start to catch on the bottom of the pan, add a splash of water and stir well. Leave the caramelized onions to cool.

When the onions are cool, beat the cream cheese, mayonnaise, and sour cream in the bowl of a stand mixer until smooth. Add the onions and the remaining bourbon and mix until combined. Chop the bacon into small pieces and add to the dip, stirring to combine. Season well with plenty of black pepper.

Spoon the dip into a 2-quart baking dish, cover, and refrigerate for several hours or overnight to allow the flavors to blend.

When ready to serve, preheat the oven to 350°. Bake the dip for 20 minutes, until it is warmed through and bubbling.

SUDDEN SUNDAYS

My grandparents' principal form of entertaining was the "Sudden Sunday." They would run into their friends at church on Sunday morning and suddenly suggest that they stop by for a drink in the evening. They'd gather for a slushy Sunday Rum Chum, a concoction of rum (lots), mint, and frozen lemonade and limeade and a spread of what my mother defines as "heavy hors d'oeuvres." Not a full meal, but enough to fill you up like one. Beaten biscuits with country ham and the cheese ring centered with strawberry or pepper jelly were frequent features. Of course, Sudden Sundays weren't really so sudden. My grandmother always prepared, getting the house clean, polishing the silver, and planning the food ahead of time. As I said, a southern lady never likes to have company without offering a "just a little something."

Deviled Egg Spread

1 dozen large eggs

¾ cup mayonnaise, preferably Duke's

2 tablespoons whole buttermilk

1 tablespoon Dijon mustard

1 tablespoon chopped parsley

½ teaspoon celery salt

½ teaspoon kosher salt

½ teaspoon sweet paprika

½ teaspoon freshly ground black pepper

Few southern parties would be complete without a tray of deviled eggs, but this rendition is less labor intensive and serves a larger crowd. In my family, it would be a sin to serve stuffed eggs (or just about anything) without a sprinkle of paprika and a garnish of parsley, so I've added that right in. Serve with crackers or toast points. This spread also makes an excellent filling for finger sandwiches.

MAKES ABOUT 2 CUPS

Place the eggs in a saucepan and cover with water. Bring the water to a boil, then cook the eggs for 7 minutes. Fill a bowl with ice cubes and water, and when the 7 minutes are up, remove the eggs to the ice water and leave until cool. Peel the eggs, rinse off any shell bits, and pat dry with paper towels.

Separate the yolks from 6 of the eggs and set the whites aside. Place the yolks and the remaining 6 whole eggs in the bowl of a food processor. Pulse a few times to break everything up. Add the remaining ingredients and pulse until smooth. Taste and add more salt if you like. Tear the reserved whites into chunks and add to the food processor. Pulse a few times to break up the whites, but leave the mixture a little chunky for texture.

Scrape the spread into a bowl, cover, and refrigerate for several hours or overnight. Sprinkle with additional paprika when serving.

Hot Pecan Country Ham Spread

This recipe is born from others—I have seen recipes in a slew of community cookbooks for hot pecan dip, and the good southern pecan lover in me has always been intrigued. But those recipes call for dried beef, which I have never used and am not sure you can still buy. It finally occurred to me to give it a try with a southern cooking staple, country ham. The result is creamy and salty and crunchy and downright delicious. This is one of those dishes that make people crowd around the buffet table.

MAKES ABOUT 3 CUPS

6 ounces center-cut country ham slices, roughly torn

3 green onions, white and light green parts, roughly chopped

2 cloves garlic

16 ounces cream cheese, softened

1 cup sour cream

½ teaspoon freshly ground black pepper

1 tablespoon unsalted butter

½ teaspoon Worcestershire sauce

1 cup chopped pecans

Place the country ham, green onions, and garlic in the bowl of a food processor. Pulse until everything is chopped to a rough purée. Scrape down the sides of the bowl and add the cream cheese, sour cream, and pepper and blend until smooth. Scrape the mixture into a 1-quart baking dish, smoothing the top.

Melt the butter in a small skillet and add the Worcestershire. Stir in the pecans and cook until the pecans are toasted and smell nice and nutty, about 5 minutes, stirring constantly. Leave the pecans to cool, then sprinkle over the top of the spread. Lightly press the pecans into the surface to adhere. The dip can be covered and refrigerated for up to 2 days at this point.

When ready to serve, preheat the oven to 350° and cook the dip until warmed through and lightly bubbling. Serve with hearty crackers.

Country Ham Pâté

4 ounces cream cheese, softened

½ cup mayonnaise, preferably Duke's

¼ cup Dijon mustard

½ teaspoon sweet paprika

A few grinds of black pepper

5 green onions, white and light green parts

1 pound ground country ham

Country Ham Pâté has the down-home goodness of salty, savory country ham, with a slightly sophisticated twist. It is easily portable and eminently useful. Try it simple, spread on crackers or corn chips, or serve it sandwiched between the halves of Cocktail Biscuits (page 158). It's great on a snacking spread with pimento cheese or other dips.

I buy ground country ham online, but you can as easily take country ham biscuit slices and pulse them to a thick paste in the food processor. I love this pâté served out of vintage canning jars, but molding it into a lovely shape adds a dash of style.

SERVES 10–12

Beat together the cream cheese, mayonnaise, mustard, paprika, and pepper until smooth in the bowl of a stand mixer. Finely chop the green onions and stir them into the mix. Crumble in the ground ham and use a sturdy wooden spoon to beat everything together until smooth and well combined.

Scrape the pâté into a bowl and refrigerate for at least 4 hours to let the flavors blend. Well covered in the fridge, this will keep for up to a week. If you want to get a little fancy, line a bowl with plastic wrap, smoothing it out as much as possible, and scoop the pâté into it. Press down on the pâté and smooth it out to remove any air pockets. Cover with plastic wrap and refrigerate until ready to use. Before serving, unwrap the top, invert the pâté onto a platter, and remove the plastic wrap.

Cheese, Please

Traditional Cheese Straws

The shatteringly crisp, ruffle-ridged cheese straw is so truly a southern staple that I had to include a classic recipe here. Charmingly pretty on a plate, standing upright in a julep cup, artfully arranged on a silver platter, or attractively packaged as a gift, nothing complements a southern cocktail better.

MAKES ABOUT 60 (CAN EASILY BE DOUBLED)

¾ cup (1½ sticks) unsalted butter, room temperature

8 ounces extra-sharp yellow cheddar cheese, grated, room temperature

2 cups all-purpose flour

½ teaspoon kosher salt, plus more for sprinkling

½ teaspoon dry mustard

¼ teaspoon cayenne pepper

Preheat the oven to 350°.

Beat the butter and the cheese in the bowl of a stand mixer until combined, then add the rest of the ingredients and beat until the mixture comes together in a ball.

If you have a cookie press, follow the manufacturer's instructions to pipe long strips of dough using the star-shaped or wavy disk onto baking sheets lined with parchment paper. Cut the strips into 2-inch pieces. Sprinkle lightly with salt.

If you don't have a cookie press, pat the dough into a flat rectangle, wrap it in plastic wrap, and refrigerate for 30 minutes. Roll the dough out into a thin sheet on a surface lightly dusted with flour. The dough should be about ¼ inch thick. Use a sharp knife or a pizza wheel to cut the dough, first into long strips, then into 2-inch ribbons. Carefully transfer the straws to baking sheets lined with parchment paper. Sprinkle lightly with salt.

Bake the straws for 13–15 minutes, until firm and lightly browned. Cool for a minute on the baking sheets, then remove to a wire rack to cool completely.

The cheese straws will keep for a week in an airtight container.

THE SOUTHERN CHEESE BOARD

The South does not have a long history of cheesemaking. But that has all begun to change, and now there are a host of amazing cheese makers producing wonderful, award-winning cheeses all over the region. Seek out local producers or order online. For information, check out the Southern Cheesemakers' Guild at www.southerncheese.com.

Here is my ultimate southern cheese board:

Dancing Fern, a soft, creamy, raw cow's milk cheese, Sequatchie Farms, Sequatchie, Tennessee

Singing Brook, a nutty, aged, hard-rind sheep's milk cheese, Blackberry Farm, Walland, Tennessee

Blackberry Blue, a herbaceous cow's milk blue, Blackberry Farm, Walland, Tennessee

Thomasville Tomme, a rich, buttery, semi-firm cow's milk cheese, Sweetgrass Dairy, Thomasville, Georgia

Green Hills, a Camembert-style double-cream cheese, Sweetgrass Dairy, Thomasville, Georgia

Ellington, an ash-rind goat cheese, Looking Glass Creamery, Asheville, North Carolina

Pecan Cheese Crisps

An easy classic, these crispy nibbles freeze for months, so you always have a homemade treat on hand. Lots of cayenne adds a good kick, and it mellows when baking.

MAKES ABOUT 36

Grate the cheese and the cold butter together on the grating blade of a food processor. Switch to the metal blade and add the flour, cayenne, and paprika. Blend until the mixture begins to come together. Add the pecans and blend until a dough forms and pulls away from the sides of the bowl. Divide the dough in half and place each piece on a length of waxed paper. Form each piece into a log and wrap tightly in the paper, twisting the ends like candy wrappers. Refrigerate until firm. The rolls can be frozen up to 6 months.

When ready to serve, preheat the oven to 350°. Remove the rolls from the fridge. If frozen, let them soften about 5 minutes. Slice into medium-thick wafers, about ¼ inch each, and place on a baking sheet lined with parchment paper or nonstick foil. Bake the slices until golden on the edges, about 12 minutes. Cool for a few minutes, then remove to a wire rack to cool.

If you would like, you can press a pecan half onto the top of each slice before baking.

8 ounces sharp yellow
   cheddar cheese
½ cup (1 stick) unsalted
   butter, cold
1½ cups all-purpose flour
1 teaspoon cayenne pepper
1 teaspoon paprika
   (preferably smoked)
2 ounces chopped pecans

Cheese Crispies

Southerners like a little cheesy bite, and there are myriad recipes for cheese coins, cheese straws, and cheese crisps. Some folks are firmly in the camp of this version, made with Rice Krispies cereal, which does add a nice little pop when eating. Don't leave out the cayenne—a little hit of heat is the secret to this recipe.

MAKES ABOUT 36

8 ounces sharp yellow cheddar cheese, grated
1 cup (2 sticks) unsalted butter, room temperature
2 cups all-purpose flour
¾ teaspoon kosher salt
¼ teaspoon cayenne pepper
2 cups Rice Krispies cereal

Beat the butter and the cheese together in the bowl of a stand mixer, then add the flour, salt, and cayenne and beat until the dough comes together in a ball. Pull the dough from the beater blade, then add the Rice Krispies and beat until combined. Knead the dough a few times by hand to bring the dough together and fully incorporate the cereal.

Divide the dough in half and place each piece on a length of waxed paper. Roll and press tightly to form 2 nice, solid logs, twisting the ends of the paper like candy wrappers. Refrigerate the logs for at least an hour before baking, but you can refrigerate them for 2 days or freeze them for up to 3 months.

When ready to bake, preheat the oven to 350° and line 2 baking sheets with parchment paper. Remove the rolls from the fridge and slice them into ¼-inch-thick wafers. Place the wafers on the baking sheet with a little room to spread, and bake until golden around the edges and firm on the top, about 10–12 minutes. Cool on the pans for a few minutes, then remove to wire racks to cool.

Williamsburg Cheese Biscuits

8 ounces sharp yellow
    cheddar cheese
1 cup (2 sticks) unsalted
    butter, room temperature
2 cups all-purpose flour
1 teaspoon kosher salt
½ teaspoon sweet paprika
¼ cup powdered sugar

I flagged this recipe in a cookbook without really reading it through because I assumed it was a recipe for traditional buttermilk biscuits with cheese. That little flag was there for years before I rediscovered it. And it is something altogether different and wonderful. Creaming the cheese with the butter creates lovely, ethereal bites, and the unusual dusting of powdered sugar adds a little mystery. Why these are called Williamsburg Cheese Biscuits I do not know. I updated it from the *Southern Sideboards Cookbook* out of Jackson, Mississippi.

MAKES ABOUT 24

Put the cheese in the bowl of a stand mixer, cover with a tea towel, and leave on the counter for 8 hours or overnight.

Preheat the oven to 450°. Line 2 baking sheets with parchment paper. Place a cooling rack on the counter set over paper or foil for easy cleanup.

Cut the cheese into chunks and place in the bowl of a stand mixer fitted with the paddle attachment. Beat the cheese for 3 minutes until smooth and light and creamy. When the cheese has been left to soften overnight, it will cream like butter. Add the butter and beat an additional 3 minutes, scraping down the sides of the bowl occasionally, until light and creamy and fluffy. Gradually add the flour, salt, and paprika. Beat until everything is combined into a cohesive dough, scraping down the sides of the bowl as necessary.

Spoon teaspoons of dough about ½ inch apart on the prepared baking sheets. I prefer to use a 1 teaspoon cookie scoop. Bake the biscuits for 8 minutes until lightly golden on the bottom and just firm on the top. I like to bake each tray separately, so that I can work quickly when sprinkling the sugar. Remove immediately to the cooling rack. Sprinkle the confectioners' sugar over the top of the hot biscuits using a sieve. You just want a light coating, so you may not use up all the sugar.

These can be served warm or at room temperature. They will keep in an airtight container for 2 days and in the freezer for a month.

Cheddar and Pepper Jelly Crumble Bars

Cheese and pepper jelly is a classic southern combination. This idea, however, was inspired by a Canadian Junior League cookbook, of all things. That recipe was for a blue cheese base with orange marmalade. The first time I read that recipe, I immediately knew I had to try it southern-style. These little jewels have become a big hit whenever I serve them.

MAKES 25

Preheat the oven to 350°. Line an 8-inch square pan with nonstick foil or foil sprayed with cooking spray.

Fit the shredding disk in a food processor and grate the cheese and the cold butter together. Switch to the metal blade, add the flour, salt, paprika, baking powder, and cayenne, and process until the mixture just starts to come together. You want clinging crumbs that easily hold together when pinched between your fingers. This may take 3 to 4 minutes. Don't let the mixture form a ball.

Reserving ½ cup of the crumbs, dump the rest into the prepared pan and press out into a flat layer with a smooth top. Spread the jelly evenly on the surface, all the way to the edges. An offset palette knife or the back of a spoon is the best tool for this. Sprinkle the remaining crumbs evenly over the pepper jelly.

Bake for 30 minutes, then remove from the oven and cool completely.

Lift out of the pan using the foil edges and cut into small squares.

You might want to label these on a buffet table or tell people what they are—someone might mistake them for strawberry crumble bars!

4 ounces extra-sharp yellow cheddar cheese
½ cup (1 stick) unsalted butter, cold
1¼ cups all-purpose flour
½ teaspoon kosher salt
½ teaspoon sweet paprika
¼ teaspoon baking powder
Dash of cayenne pepper
1 (10.5-ounce) jar red pepper jelly (such as Braswell's)

Pepper Jelly Pimento Cheese

1 cup mayonnaise,
  preferably Duke's
¼ cup red pepper jelly
  (such as Braswell's)
1 tablespoon apple cider
  vinegar
½ teaspoon sweet paprika
½ teaspoon kosher salt
Generous grinds of black
  pepper
1 (4-ounce) jar diced
  pimentos, rinsed and
  drained
8 ounces extra-sharp yellow
  cheddar cheese
8 ounces extra-sharp white
  cheddar cheese

Pimento cheese is for me the ultimate southern snack. And I literally wrote the book on pimento cheese. While I was researching and developing *Pimento Cheese: The Cookbook*, I came across lots of recipes and had many people tell me that they like a little sugar in the mix. I tried, but I never really warmed to the granulated sugar idea. While racking my brain for another way to make the spread for this book, it hit me—why not stir in a little sweet-tart pepper jelly? I serve pimento cheese with homemade pepper jelly for dolloping, and I love a sandwich with some PC and pepper jelly, so it is actually kind of an obvious twist. And this little note of sweetness I really like.

MAKES ABOUT 3 CUPS

Whisk the mayonnaise, pepper jelly, vinegar, paprika, salt, and pepper together in a large bowl until well combined. You want to make sure there are no big lumps in the jelly, so use a fork or a whisk if needed. Stir in the pimentos.

Grate the cheeses in the food processor fitted with the grating disk or on the large holes of a box grater. Add to the bowl with the mayo mixture and stir to combine, making sure you separate the strands of cheese and get them coated with mayonnaise. Cover and refrigerate for several hours to let the flavors blend.

Classic Cheese Ring with Strawberry Preserves

The cheese ring with preserves is a true southern classic, one that has appeared on holiday tables as long as the living can remember. I had forgotten about this, until I was checking out at the beauty shop one day and overheard a conversation about an upcoming holiday party. I heard, "What are you bringing?" and the answer was, "That cheese ring." "Oh, the one with the strawberry jelly? I love that . . . you know, I think I'll make that for book club."

SERVES 10–12

Line a 6-cup ring mold with plastic wrap. Do your very best to press the plastic directly onto the surface of the mold with no bubbles beneath the wrap. Leave a generous overhang of wrap.

Stir the mayonnaise, paprika, salt, black pepper, and cayenne together in a bowl. Grate the cheese on the fine holes of a box grater into the bowl. Finely chop the green onions and the garlic and add to the bowl. Tumble in the pecans and stir well until everything is thoroughly combined. Make sure the cheese and the mayo are well mixed and everything is evenly distributed so that the cheese ring will serve nicely.

Use your good clean hands to press a layer of the cheese mix into the bottom of the mold and press down firmly and evenly. This helps to ensure that the top of the ring is even when unmolded. Press in the rest of the cheese mixture, packing it in firmly and evenly. Pull the overlapping plastic to cover the top, and press down again to make sure that the cheese is really packed in there.

Refrigerate the mold for at least 6 hours, but overnight is best. You can also make the ring up to 3 days ahead and keep it covered in the mold in the fridge.

When ready to serve, unwrap the top of the cheese, invert the ring onto a platter, and lift off the mold. Carefully remove the plastic wrap. Fill the center of the ring with strawberry preserves

¾ cup mayonnaise, preferably Duke's
½ teaspoon sweet paprika
½ teaspoon kosher salt
½ teaspoon freshly ground black pepper
Dash of cayenne pepper
1 pound extra-sharp cheddar cheese
3 green onions, white and light green parts
1 clove garlic
1 cup finely chopped pecans
Strawberry preserves

(how much you use will depend on the size of the well in the center of your ring). Serve with crackers.

Don't have a ring mold? Line a large round bowl with plastic wrap and pack the cheese into it. When you unmold the cheese, you can either pour the preserves over the top, letting them drip down over the sides, or use a round spoon and your fingers to press a well into the center of the cheese ball and fill that with preserves. Serve additional preserves in a small bowl on the side.

DERBY DAY RECIPES

Benedictine

Hot Pecan Country
    Ham Spread

Country Ham
    Cheesecake

Kentucky Beer Cheese

Kentucky Hot Brown
    Bites

Devils on Muleback
    (Pecan-Stuffed
    Dates Wrapped in
    Country Ham)

Pecan Biscuits with
    Ham and Bourbon
    Mayonnaise

DERBY DAY

The Kentucky Derby is one of the most iconic of southern celebrations. The first Saturday in May, crowds descend on Churchill Downs in Louisville to watch the racing. Ok, maybe it's to show off fantastical hats and perfectly tailored seersucker suits or to gawk at the other attendees in their marvelous attire or to celebrity spot. Okay, it is also to drink mint juleps and sing "My Old Kentucky Home" half in the bag. But any event with that scope of tradition lends itself to over-the-top celebrations. Southerners do love a good theme party. Derby parties are also a tradition all over the South for those who can't make it to the event itself. Women still wear hats, men seersucker suits. It's a chance to pull out the julep cups and the heirloom linen cocktail napkins. The race itself is known as the Greatest Two Minutes in Sports, but the parties last for hours.

Bacon Pecan Cheese Ball

The cheese ball gets a bad rap. Maybe people have memories of those shrink-wrapped, shelf-stable, processed cheese lumps that came in the Christmas gift box from the bank or the insurance company. But a homemade cheese ball is a different thing all together, and well worth making. And of course, bacon makes everything better, so this version is definitely a keeper.

MAKES 1

Preheat the oven to 400°. Place a wire rack inside a rimmed baking sheet and arrange the bacon strips on the rack. Cook the bacon until very crispy, 20–25 minutes. Pat the bacon strips on both sides with paper towels to blot off any fat. Leave to cool.

Break 5 strips bacon into pieces and place in the bowl of a food processor fitted with the metal blade. Add ½ cup of the pecan halves and the parsley. Process until the bacon and pecans are the texture of coarse bread crumbs. Scoop the crumbs out onto a flat plate.

Switch to the grating blade and grate the cheddar cheese. Switch back to the metal blade, add the cream cheese, cut into cubes, the remaining bacon, broken into pieces, the remaining pecans, the bacon grease, and the chives, salt, and paprika. Process until smooth and all the ingredients are incorporated, scraping down the sides of the bowl as necessary.

Use your good clean hands to shape the cheese mixture into a ball, then roll the ball in the bacon crumbs, pressing them into the sides of the ball. Refrigerate until firm. The cheese ball can be made up to 3 days ahead.

If you want to be fancy, you can roll the mixture into small "truffles" and serve with toothpicks.

10 strips of bacon
1 cup pecan halves, divided
2 tablespoons parsley
8 ounces extra-sharp cheddar cheese
8 ounces cream cheese, room temperature
2 tablespoons snipped chives
1 tablespoon bacon grease
1 teaspoon kosher salt
½ teaspoon sweet paprika
¼ teaspoon cayenne pepper

Country Ham Cheesecake

1 sleeve buttery crackers (such as Townhouse), about 34 crackers

½ cup chopped pecans

½ cup (1 stick) unsalted butter, melted

6 ounces center-cut country ham biscuit slices

4 green onions, white and light green parts

1 clove garlic

16 ounces cream cheese, softened

2 large eggs

1¼ cups sour cream

8 ounces sharp white cheddar cheese, grated

2 teaspoons Worcestershire sauce

1 teaspoon hot sauce (such as Crystal)

1 teaspoon kosher salt

Generous grinds of black pepper

Savory cheesecakes are a thing. I've had them at parties all my life. When I submitted the manuscript for *Pimento Cheese: The Cookbook* to my New York–based publisher, the editors and copy editors were sure that a pimento cheese cheesecake would cause great confusion. When I first conceived this salty, savory, country ham version, I knew it would be good, but in truth, it is better than good. It even surprised me. The added bonus of this treat is that it serves a crowd. And a little pepper jelly on the side is not a bad thing.

SERVES A CROWD

Preheat the oven to 350°. Spray a 9-inch springform pan with nonstick spray. Wrap a piece of foil around the bottom of the pan to catch any dripping butter from the crust.

Process the crackers and pecans to fine crumbs in a small food processor. Add the melted butter and process until it all comes together. It will be very wet—don't worry. Press the crumbs onto the bottom of the springform pan, pressing a little bit up the sides of the pan. Bake the crust for 10 minutes, then remove to a wire rack to cool.

Wipe out the food processor bowl, then add the ham pieces, green onions, and garlic and pulse to chop everything very finely. You want all the ingredients chopped but not blended to a paste.

Beat the cream cheese, eggs, and sour cream together in the bowl of a stand mixer until smooth. Add the grated cheddar and beat until combined. Add the Worcestershire, hot sauce, salt, and pepper. Beat in the ham mixture until evenly distributed and combined.

Spread the filling evenly over the crust, smoothing the top. Bake the cheesecake for 30 minutes, until completely firm and lightly browned on top. Cool in the pan on a wire rack, then chill in the refrigerator, loosely covered, for several hours or overnight. When ready to serve, release the springform ring and transfer the cheesecake to a platter.

Serve with crackers.

FOUR WAYS WITH A
BLOCK OF CREAM CHEESE

At every Christmas function in my youth someone who had been asked to bring an appetizer would sail into the kitchen in her party dress and clacky high heels with her most festive Christmas plate and a spreading knife, sometimes all tucked away in a basket with a colorful napkin. Talking a mile a minute, undoubtedly, she'd pull out her plate, unwrap a block of cream cheese, plop it down—just the block, as is. Out came the jar with its hand-written label and little fabric cap tied with a gold stretchy cord. Its contents were poured over the cream cheese and served with crackers. That was that. What was in the jar varied, sometimes homemade, sometimes store-bought, or a quick combination of the two.

Jezebel Jelly

1 (12-ounce) jar apricot jelly
1 (12-ounce) jar pineapple preserves
1 (5-ounce) jar prepared horseradish
1 (1.38-ounce) jar dry mustard (½ cup)
Generous grinds of black pepper

My version is adapted from several recipe cards I found tucked in a drawer. I think they came from my mother, but they are not in her handwriting. Traditions do pass around.

MAKES ABOUT 4 CUPS (OR 4 HALF-PINT JARS)

In a medium bowl, mix the apricot jelly and pineapple preserves until smooth and combined. I like to use a hand mixer, but you can stir vigorously with a spoon. Blend in the horseradish until combined, then sift in the mustard and mix to combine. I highly recommend sifting the mustard. This jelly has got enough kick without a lump of mustard in each bite. Grind in lots of black pepper, and stir to combine.

Leave the jelly in the bowl for an hour or so to blend the flavors, then scoop into airtight jars or containers and refrigerate. The jelly will last for a month in the fridge.

Praline Sauce

Before baked brie became the rage, there was this tangy, sweet-salty combo of pecans and brown sugar. It is amazing paired with rich cream cheese.

½ cup (1 stick) unsalted
butter
½ cup dark brown sugar
1 teaspoon Worcestershire
sauce
1 teaspoon yellow mustard
¾ cup chopped pecans

MAKES ABOUT 2 CUPS

Combine the butter, sugar, Worcestershire, and mustard in a small saucepan and heat over medium heat until the sugar has dissolved, about 5 minutes. Let the sauce come just to a bubble and stir until the sugar is no longer grainy. Stir in the pecans and remove from the heat. Leave to cool, then spoon over the cream cheese.

Pepper Jelly

Homemade, store-bought, or a gift from a friend. Red or green, sweet or hot. Pepper jelly is an iconic southern condiment used to glaze meat, jazz up vegetables, or brighten a sandwich. But poured over a block of cream cheese is probably the most common use for a good pepper jelly.

Pickapeppa Sauce

I can't imagine how Jamaican Pickapeppa Sauce become a food trend in the South, but a block of cream cheese coated with a bottle has long been a popular "cheats" appetizer. It covers the bases—a piquant, tangy sauce over the rich creamy cheese. Pickapeppa Sauce is a muddy brown color, so this version of a cream cheese appetizer is not the most attractive dish on the table, but it is invariably scraped clean.

Kentucky Beer Cheese

1 pound extra-sharp
  cheddar cheese
½ cup (1 stick) unsalted
  butter
1 clove garlic
2 tablespoons
  Worcestershire sauce
1 teaspoon white wine
  vinegar
1 teaspoon dry mustard
½ teaspoon smoked
  paprika
½ teaspoon hot sauce
  (such as Crystal)
½ cup beer, preferably lager

There is just nothing bad about beer and cheese together. This tangy spread is tailgating heaven, and of course, good for a Derby Day party. I have yet to discover why beer cheese is a product of the land of bourbon, but I'm not complaining.

MAKES ABOUT 3 CUPS

Cut the cheese and the butter into small cubes and place in the bowl of a food processor fitted with the metal blade. Leave to come to room temperature. Add the garlic and process until smooth. Add the Worcestershire, vinegar, mustard, paprika, and hot sauce and process to combine. With the motor running, pour in the beer and process until smooth and creamy. Scrape the beer cheese into a bowl, cover, and refrigerate for several hours to let the flavors blend. The beer cheese will keep in the fridge for 5 days. Serve with hearty crackers.

Deep-Fried Love

THE HOLLYWOOD

For the past twenty years or so, Tunica, Mississippi, has been largely known as a gaming destination. There are casinos rising out of the flat, flat Delta—suddenly skyscrapers loom in the distance. But long before that, Tunica was a small Delta farming community with a pretty town square surrounded by acres of cotton fields. And right outside Tunica is the Hollywood Café, in an old farm commissary building. When I was young, before the casinos, it was a special event to drive about an hour and half down Highway 61 in the deep Delta dark to have dinner at the Hollywood. Fried dill pickles, catfish, and frozen brandy Alexanders. There were always musicians, a female piano player on Fridays, a guitarist on Saturdays. A big table of friends would eat, drink, and sing along, loudly and badly, particularly to Hank Williams Jr.'s "Family Traditions." A friend and I rented a bus to drive a group to the Hollywood on a college break. One fellow crashed the party, he met a girl, and they had their rehearsal dinner at the Hollywood (and they are still married).

The Hollywood is still there, though the four-lane highway and casino traffic have taken some of the luster out of the late-night adventure. I haven't been in ages, but as I write this, I know I have to plan a trip soon.

I tell this story because the Hollywood's main claim to fame is that they invented the fried dill pickle in 1969. I have no hard-and-fast evidence to prove this, but that's their story and I'm sticking to it. They serve theirs as thin chips, never spears, which is in my opinion the only way.

Hollywood Fried Dill Pickles

This recipe, from a proprietor of the Hollywood Café, appears in *A Man's Taste*, a cookbook published by the Junior League of Memphis and spearheaded by, of all people, my dad. The recipe contributors were all men, and the food and skill level required generally reflects that fact.

SERVES 6–8

4 large dill pickles
½ cup all-purpose flour
1 tablespoon cayenne pepper
1 tablespoon sweet paprika
1 tablespoon freshly ground black pepper
1 teaspoon kosher salt
¼ cup beer, preferably lager
Vegetable oil for frying

Slice the pickles into chips about ¼ inch thick. Do not use presliced pickle chips; they will be too soggy.

Pour 2 inches of oil into a deep, heavy pot and attach a candy thermometer. Heat over medium-high heat to 375°. Place a rimmed baking sheet lined with a cooling rack near the stovetop.

While the oil is heating, whisk the flour, cayenne, paprika, pepper, and salt together in a large bowl. Whisk in the beer to make a smooth batter.

When the oil is hot, dip each pickle slice separately into the batter, turning it around to get fully coated. Shake off excess batter and drop into the oil. Fry until the pickles float to the surface and are golden brown, about 4 minutes. Remove cooked pickles to the rack-lined baking sheet. Repeat with all the pickles. Do not crowd the pan when frying, so the pickles have room to float.

The pickles can be kept warm in a 300° oven for about 15 minutes.

Comeback Sauce

½ cup mayonnaise,
preferably Duke's
¼ cup vegetable oil
¼ cup chili sauce
2 tablespoons ketchup
2 teaspoons stone-ground
mustard
2 teaspoons Worcestershire
sauce
Dash hot sauce (such as
Crystal)
2 cloves garlic
½ small white onion or
1 small shallot
1 teaspoon kosher salt
1 teaspoon freshly ground
black pepper

Comeback Sauce is a specialty of Jackson, Mississippi. It apparently originated in Greek restaurants and is now found on restaurant tables all over the city. It really hasn't made its way up to Memphis, but as you meander through the Delta, you do find it on some restaurant menus. That's where I discovered it. And of course, it shows up in community cookbooks in many forms with many uses. This is my version. Comeback Sauce is wonderful with all manner of fried things.

MAKES 2 CUPS

Place all the ingredients in a blender and blend until smooth and combined. Pour into an airtight container and refrigerate for 24 hours to allow the flavors to marry. The sauce will keep in the fridge for a week.

Serve Comeback Sauce with Fried Dill Pickles, Fried Okra, Corn Fritters, or Catfish Bites. It is also a great dip for chips or vegetables and an excellent addition to a burger or a sandwich.

Fried Okra

High on the list of poppable southern snacks come little nuggets of crispy fried okra. And yes, fried okra makes the perfect starter to a fried catfish basket, so you will usually find it on the menu at a fish camp. Eat these straight up or serve them with Comeback Sauce (opposite) or Remoulade Sauce (page 70) for dipping.

SERVES 6-8

1 pound okra
2 cups whole buttermilk
1 cup all-purpose flour
1 cup yellow cornmeal
2 teaspoons kosher salt
½ teaspoon freshly ground
    black pepper
¼ teaspoon cayenne
    pepper
Vegetable oil for frying

Remove the stem and the tip from the okra and slice into ½-inch pieces. Place in a large bowl and pour over the buttermilk. Stir to coat the okra, then refrigerate for 45 minutes to an hour.

When ready to cook the okra, line a rimmed baking sheet with paper towels and place a wire rack on top. Pour 2 inches of oil into a deep, heavy pot and attach a candy thermometer. Heat over medium-high heat to 375°. While the oil is heating, stir together the flour, cornmeal, salt, and peppers in a large bowl until combined. Drain the okra through a colander, then add to the flour mixture a handful at a time. Toss to coat each piece of okra evenly in the flour, then drop it into the hot oil and fry until golden brown, about 4 minutes. Remove to the prepared rack and repeat with the remaining okra. Serve immediately.

Corn Fritters with Spicy Honey

Crispy, crunchy corn fritters are a personal favorite; add a little sweet fire and you've really got me. The spicy honey really is hot—you can take it down to one chile or up it to three—and it has an amazing host of uses. Try it drizzled over fried chicken or roasted sweet potatoes.

MAKES ABOUT 24

For the spicy honey, pour the honey into a small saucepan. Finely slice the chiles and add to the honey. Stir in the vinegar and heat the honey over medium-low heat until it is barely simmering. Reduce the heat to low and cook for an hour to fully infuse the honey. Watch carefully so the honey does not start bubbling or boiling. Let the honey sit for 30 minutes off the heat, then strain through a fine-mesh strainer into an airtight jar. Cool completely before covering. The honey will keep in a cool, dark place for up to 2 months.

For the fritters, combine the flour, cornmeal, baking powder, salt, and pepper together in a medium mixing bowl and stir to combine. Add the egg, milk, and honey and beat until thoroughly combined and smooth. Stir in the corn until evenly distributed.

Pour 4 inches of oil in a deep, heavy pot. Clip on a candy thermometer and heat over high heat to 375°. Scoop tablespoonfuls of batter into the hot oil. I like to use a small cookie scoop, which makes perfectly lovely, evenly sized, round fritters, but you can also scoop with a tablespoon and scrape the batter into the oil with a second spoon. Fry until the fritters are floating, and dark golden brown, 3–4 minutes. Try one first and time how long it takes to cook through. Don't crowd the pot—make sure there is plenty of room to flip the fritters over. Remove the fritters with a slotted spoon to a baking sheet lined with paper towels. Repeat with all the batter, making sure the oil remains between 350° and 360°.

Serve immediately drizzled with hot spicy honey.

FOR THE SPICY HONEY
1 cup honey
2 Fresno chiles
1 tablespoon apple cider vinegar

FOR THE CORN FRITTERS
¾ cup all-purpose flour
2 tablespoons yellow cornmeal
1½ teaspoons baking powder
1 teaspoon kosher salt
½ teaspoon freshly ground black pepper
1 large egg
½ cup whole milk
1 tablespoon spicy honey, regular honey, or granulated sugar
2 cups corn kernels, from 2 ears of corn or frozen, thawed and drained
Vegetable oil for frying

Fried Grits with Tomato-Bacon Jam

This is how you serve grits as a snack: crispy little fried squares with a dollop of sweet and smoky tomato-bacon jam.

MAKES ABOUT 25 SQUARES AND 1 PINT JAM

For the jam, cut the bacon into small pieces and cook in a skillet until crispy. Transfer with a slotted spoon to paper towels to drain.

In a large, high-sided saucepan, bring the chopped tomatoes, onions, sugars, vinegar, salt, and pepper to a boil. Boil for about 10 minutes, until the tomatoes are soft and breaking down. Use a spatula or the back of the spoon to crush the tomatoes; I like to give the jam a little whirl with an immersion blender to create a rough purée. Reduce the heat to medium-low, stir in the bacon pieces, and simmer until the jam is thick and spreadable, about an hour or more. Stir occasionally to prevent scorching on the bottom of the pan. As the jam thickens, watch it more closely and stir often to prevent burning. The jam is done when you pull a spatula through to expose the bottom of the pan and the two sides don't run together.

Scoop the jam into a jar or a bowl and leave to cool. The jam will keep covered in the fridge for more than a week.

For the grits, stir the milk, water, butter, hot sauce, and salt together in a large Dutch oven and bring to a boil over medium-high heat. Slowly whisk in the grits, then lower the heat and simmer until the grits are very tender, about an hour. Stir occasionally to prevent catching on the bottom of the pan. When the grits are cooked, stir in the cheese until melted and smooth. Line a 9 × 13-inch rimmed baking pan with nonstick foil or parchment paper, with some hanging over the ends. Spread the grits in the pan in an even layer, about 1 inch thick. Leave to cool completely. The grits can be made a day ahead, covered, and refrigerated.

Use the overhanging foil to lift the grits from the pan and cut into 1-inch squares. Put a little all-purpose flour seasoned with salt and pepper in a bowl and toss the grits squares around with your

FOR THE TOMATO-BACON JAM
6 strips of bacon
2 pounds tomatoes, chopped
1 small white onion, finely chopped
½ cup granulated sugar
½ cup light brown sugar
3 tablespoons apple cider vinegar
1 teaspoon kosher salt
½ teaspoon freshly ground black pepper

FOR THE GRITS
2 cups whole milk
2 cups water
¼ cup (½ stick) unsalted butter
2 teaspoons hot sauce (such as Crystal)
2 teaspoons kosher salt
1 cup stone-ground yellow grits
½ cup grated cheddar cheese
All-purpose flour
Kosher salt and freshly ground black pepper
Vegetable oil for frying

fingers until lightly coated. Place the coated squares on a plate. Pour 2 inches of oil into a deep, heavy pot and attach a candy thermometer. Heat over medium-high heat to 375°. Fry the grits squares until golden and crispy, about 2 minutes, flipping them over during cooking. Remove with a slotted spoon to a plate lined with paper towels.

Serve the grits squares warm with a dollop of tomato-bacon jam.

FAIR FOOD

The South excels at the great American tradition of the state or county fair. Our fairs certainly offer the universal fair food classics, including corn dogs, funnel cakes, and turkey legs, but never ones to miss an opportunity to be different, southern food vendors have created a host of wildly inventive specialties. And fried is the specialty of any fair. The huge Texas State Fair is infamous for its fried foods. Texans will fry anything. Butter, yep, been there, done that. Fried chicken pot pie, you bet. Fried Jell-O. Fried Jell-O, people. The North Carolina State Fair once featured fried Pop-Tarts. At the State Fair of Virginia, you could wash down your deep-fried brownie or chocolate chip cookie with a glass of bacon iced tea. You can beat the heat at the Florida State Fair with a burger topped with deep-fried ice cream. Though I am not sure why you'd want to. Snack on a fried peanut butter and jelly sandwich at the Alabama National Fair while strolling the midway. The Neshoba County Fair in Philadelphia, Mississippi, features brightly painted cabins, passed down from generation to generation, which the owners settle in for fair week. There's a lot of home cooking going on, but it's Mississippi after all, so folks step out for fried catfish, fried chicken, fried okra, fried green tomatoes . . . you get the picture. It's also a well-known venue for serious politicking, and nobody wants to do that on an empty stomach.

Catfish Bites with Beer Sauce

The fried catfish basket is perhaps the most iconic (and only) seafood-related dish in the landlocked parts of the South, particularly Mississippi, where the landscape is now dotted with commercial catfish farms. Fried is the best way to eat catfish, and serving it in little dippable nuggets makes a perfect snack. Oh, and it never hurts to dip them in beer.

SERVES 6–8

For the catfish, cut the fish fillets into 1-inch chunks and place in a large zip-top bag. Pour over the buttermilk and add the hot sauce. Squish everything around to blend and coat the catfish. Place the bag on a plate to catch any drips, then refrigerate for at least 8 hours or overnight.

When ready to cook, line a rimmed baking sheet with paper towels and place a wire rack on top. Pour the catfish pieces into a colander and leave to drain for about 15 minutes. Pour 2 inches of oil into a deep, heavy pot and attach a candy thermometer. Heat over medium-high heat to 360°. Place the cornmeal, flour, salt, and pepper into a large zip-top plastic bag and shake to combine. Drop a handful of the catfish pieces into the coating and shake to coat each piece thoroughly. Drop the fish into the oil a chunk at a time, being sure not to crowd the pan. Fry until the fish is browned and floats to the top, about 4 minutes, then remove to the wire rack. Repeat with the remaining chunks. You can keep the fish warm in a 225° oven for 15 minutes before serving if needed.

For the beer sauce, put the mustard and the beer in the carafe of a blender. Blend for a few seconds to combine. Drop in the onion pieces, add the Worcestershire, hot sauce, and mayonnaise, and blend until completely smooth and combined. Transfer to a bowl, cover, and refrigerate for several hours. This is best made a day ahead but can be made up to 3 days in advance.

FOR THE FISH

- 2 pounds catfish fillets
- 2 cups whole buttermilk
- 1 tablespoon hot sauce (such as Crystal)
- 1½ cups yellow cornmeal
- ⅔ cup all-purpose flour
- 2 teaspoons kosher salt
- 2 teaspoons freshly ground black pepper
- Vegetable oil for frying

FOR THE BEER SAUCE

- 1 (1.38-ounce) jar dry mustard (½ cup)
- ½ cup beer, preferably lager
- 3 green onions, white and light green parts, chopped
- 1 tablespoon Worcestershire sauce
- 1 tablespoon hot sauce (such as Crystal)
- 2 cups mayonnaise, preferably Duke's

Squash Puppies

1 cups whole buttermilk
2 large eggs
2 cups yellow cornmeal
¾ cup self-rising flour
1 tablespoon granulated
  sugar
3 teaspoons baking powder
2 teaspoons finely chopped
  fresh thyme
1½ teaspoons kosher salt
½ teaspoon freshly ground
  black pepper
2 medium yellow summer
  squash (about 1 pound),
  finely minced
2 green onions, light and
  light green parts, finely
  minced
Canola oil for frying

The southern garden pumps out summer squash like there's no tomorrow. As a result, southerners have learned a million ways to use the sunny-tinged, swan-necked lovelies to best advantage. I planned a wedding one time on a beautiful property complete with caged-in gardens. Every time I met with the parents, the father of the bride sent me home with grocery sacks full of squash. It seems only natural when summer fish-fry season is in full swing to stir some squash into the classic hushpuppies. These little nuggets make a great snack with Comeback Sauce (page 000). I slice the squash into rounds, then stack the rounds and cut them into a grid of small pieces. You can pulse chunks in the food processor, but if any liquid is produced, drain it off.

MAKES ABOUT 24

Beat the buttermilk with the eggs in large bowl until combined, then add the cornmeal, flour, sugar, baking powder, thyme, salt, and pepper and stir until everything is combined, with no dry ingredients visible in the bowl. Fold in the finely minced squash and green onions just until evenly distributed. I find it easiest to use my good clean hands at the end to get everything together. Set the batter aside at room temperature for about 15 minutes to rest.

Pour 4 inches of oil in a deep, heavy pot. Clip on a candy thermometer and heat over high heat to 375°. Scoop ping-pong balls of batter into the hot oil. I like to use a small cookie scoop, which makes lovely, evenly sized, round puppies, but you can also scoop with a tablespoon and scrape the batter into the oil with a second spoon. Fry until the puppies are floating and dark golden brown, about 2–3 minutes. Try one first and time how long it takes to cook through. Don't crowd the pot—make sure there is plenty of room to flip the puppies over. Remove the puppies with a slotted spoon to a baking sheet lined with paper towels. Repeat with all the batter, making sure the oil remains between 350° and 360°. You can keep the puppies warm in a 225° oven for 15 minutes before serving.

Calas with Charred Green Onion Dip

Calas are an old New Orleans specialty. These little fried rice fritters were once sold on the street by women carrying them in baskets on their head shouting, "Calas tout chaud!" (hot calas) to announce their arrival. Women of African descent, from the time of slavery through the civil rights era, often turned to food in building their own economies. Traditionally, calas are served covered in powdered sugar, much like a beignet, but I think they make a wonderful savory snack with this smoky charred green onion sauce for dipping. Sure, these take a little patience, but the result is a truly unique bite.

MAKES ABOUT 16 CALAS AND 2 CUPS DIP

For the sauce, cut the roots from the green onions and discard, then cut the thicker white and light green parts off. Cut about 6 inches off the green tops, discarding any dried or brown ends. Brush or spray all the pieces with olive oil. Heat a grill or grill pan over high heat. Put all the green onion pieces on the grill and cook until charred and browned all over, about 15 minutes in all. The thin green tops will cook faster; remove them to a plate as they brown. The thicker white parts will take longer. Remove the charred onions to a plate to cool.

Place the charred onions in the bowl of a food processor (a mini is fine) and pulse to chop finely, scraping down the sides of the bowl as needed. Add the sour cream, mayonnaise, hot sauce, salt, and pepper and blend until smooth and well combined. Pour the sauce into a bowl, cover, and refrigerate for several hours to allow the flavors to blend. The sauce can be made up to 2 days ahead.

For the calas, pour 1½ cups of water into a saucepan with a tight-fitting lid, then stir in the rice. Bring to a boil and continue boiling until almost all the water is absorbed by the rice and little air bubbles form on the surface of the rice, about 10–12 minutes, stirring a few times to prevent sticking. Remove from the heat and tightly cover the pan. Set aside for 15 minutes, then fluff with a fork. (This makes a little more rice than you need for the calas.)

FOR THE DIP
16 green onions
Olive oil
1 cup sour cream
½ cup mayonnaise, preferably Duke's
2 teaspoons hot sauce (such as Crystal)
1 teaspoon kosher salt
½ teaspoon freshly ground black pepper

FOR THE CALAS
½ cup long-grain white rice
1 package (.25 ounces) active dry yeast
1 tablespoon granulated sugar
¾ cup all-purpose flour
2 large eggs
½ teaspoon kosher salt

Whisk the yeast and sugar together in a large bowl, then add ½ cup of warm water and whisk to combine. Leave the yeast to sit for 10 minutes until foamy and bubbling, then stir in 1 cup of cooked, lukewarm rice until combined. Cover the bowl with plastic wrap and leave at room temperature 8 hours or overnight.

At least an hour before you are ready to serve the calas, stir the flour, eggs, and salt into the rice mixture until smooth and well combined. Cover the bowl again and leave for an hour to rise. The batter should be about as thick as pancake batter.

Pour 4 inches of oil in a deep, heavy pot. Clip on a candy thermometer and heat over high heat to 375°. Scoop tablespoons full of batter into the hot oil. I like to use a small cookie scoop, but you can also scoop with a tablespoon and scrape the batter into the oil with a second spoon. Fry until the fritters are floating, and dark golden brown, 3–4 minutes. Try one first and time how long it takes to cook through. Don't crowd the pot—make sure there is plenty of room to flip the calas over. Remove the fritters with a slotted spoon to a baking sheet lined with paper towels. Repeat with all the batter, making sure the oil remains between 350° and 360°.

Seafood and Eat It

Crab Cake Bites with Artichoke Tartar Sauce

I fiddled with a classic crab cake recipe, paring it down to basic flavors so the tartar sauce wouldn't be overwhelmed. And pressing the mixture into little muffin tins makes the cakes easier to cook and perfect bites for a party—the tins can be filled and refrigerated until ready to bake. A little dollop of tartar sauce makes them pretty, and the mini-sized, crispy sides make them easy to eat.

MAKES 24 CRAB CAKES AND ABOUT 2 CUPS SAUCE

For the crab cakes, beat the eggs in a large bowl. Pick over the crabmeat to make sure there are no pieces of shell, then add the crab to the eggs. Add the melted butter, mayonnaise, and parsley and fold together gently. You want everything well combined, but try not to break up the crabmeat too much.

Mix the bread crumbs, baking powder, Old Bay, and dry mustard together in a small bowl. Add to the crab mixture and gently fold through. Again, you want everything combined, but don't break up the crabmeat. Refrigerate the mixture for at least an hour, and several is fine. This binds the mixture together and makes it easier to fill the tins.

Preheat the oven to 350°. Spray 24 mini-muffin cups well with nonstick cooking spray. Fill each cup with crab cake mixture, pressing it in to fill each cavity to the top. Press a rounded teaspoon down in the middle of each cake to make a little well in the center (this will keep them from mounding up and create a nice, flat surface for the tartar sauce). You can cover the tins with plastic wrap and keep them in the fridge for several hours at this point.

Bake the crab cakes for 20–25 minutes, until golden brown, then cool in the pan for 5 minutes. Use a knife to loosen the cakes and remove them from the pan. Spoon a little tartar sauce on top of each cake and serve immediately, though these also taste lovely at room temperature.

For the tartar sauce, drain and rinse the artichoke hearts well and pat dry. Drop them in a food processor (I use the mini) and add the capers, egg yolks, parsley, and garlic. Pulse 3 or 4 times to

FOR THE CRAB CAKES
2 large eggs
1 pound lump crabmeat (see note)
2 tablespoons butter, melted and cooled
1 tablespoon mayonnaise, preferably Duke's
1 tablespoon finely chopped flat-leaf parsley
½ cup panko bread crumbs
1 teaspoon baking powder
1 teaspoon Old Bay Seasoning
½ teaspoon dry mustard

FOR THE TARTAR SAUCE
4 medium whole artichoke hearts (see Note)
2 egg yolks
2 cloves garlic
2 tablespoons flat-leaf parsley leaves
2 tablespoons capers, rinsed and drained
¼ cup neutral oil (such as vegetable, grapeseed, or canola)

break everything up into a rough paste; scrape down the sides of the bowl. With the motor running, drizzle the oil into the bowl in a thin, steady stream. Process until the sauce is thick and creamy. Stop to scrape down the sides of the bowl halfway through. Scrape the tartar sauce into a container and keep covered in the fridge until ready to use. It will keep overnight.

Note: I prefer pasteurized lump crabmeat that I find in containers at the seafood counter at better grocery stores. I generally use canned artichoke hearts in brine instead of the marinated, quartered ones in jars because the marinated ones have some flavor additions. If you can only find those, rinse them really well. If you can only find quartered, use 12 quarters.

Shrimp Paste

Not the most appealing name for a recipe, but it is a classic of the Charleston cooking canon. For many years, I made this as instructed by the grandmother of a friend—just cooked shrimp, butter, mace, and splash of sherry put through a grinder. I, of course, use the food processor. I eventually changed up my recipe, inspired by the doyenne of southern cooking, Edna Lewis, who cooked for many years at Middleton Place plantation outside Charleston. This version creates a luxuriously decadent paste. I use this for very delicate and ladylike tea sandwiches or serve it as a spread with toast points.

MAKES 2 CUPS

1 cup (2 sticks) unsalted butter, softened and divided
1 pound small pink shrimp, peeled and deveined
¼ cup dry sherry
2 tablespoons fresh lemon juice
½ teaspoon kosher salt
½ teaspoon freshly ground black pepper
¼ teaspoon sweet paprika
¼ teaspoon ground mace

Melt 6 tablespoons of the butter in a skillet over medium-high heat until it is foaming, then add the shrimp. Cook, stirring frequently, until the shrimp are cooked through and pink, about 5 minutes. Use a slotted spoon to transfer the shrimp to the bowl of a food processor fitted with the metal blade, leaving the butter behind in the pan. Add the sherry and the lemon juice to the pan and cook until reduced to 3 tablespoons, about 5 minutes. Measure the 3 tablespoons carefully or the paste will be too loose.

While the liquid is reducing, add the salt, pepper, paprika, and mace to the shrimp in the food processor and pulse to break up the shrimp. Add the reduced liquid and pulse until combined. With the machine running, add the remaining softened butter a tablespoon at a time, mixing well after each addition. Blend until smooth and creamy. Scrape the paste into a container, cool, and cover.

The shrimp paste will keep, covered and refrigerated, for up to a week.

Citrus Pickled Shrimp

1 navel orange
1 lemon
1 lime
¼ cup mixed citrus juice
1 cup white vinegar
½ cup olive oil
2 tablespoons capers
    in brine
1 clove garlic, minced
1 teaspoon celery salt
1 teaspoon red pepper
    flakes
1 teaspoon kosher salt
2 bay leaves
3-4 sprigs fresh rosemary
2 pounds large shrimp,
    peeled and deveined

Pickled shrimp are a classic party dish and a beach vacation treat. Easy to make ahead or to have on hand for snacking, the pretty pink shrimp look beautiful in a cut crystal dish or a big ol' Mason jar. I've amped up my traditional pickled shrimp recipe with mixed citrus and a light hit of rosemary.

SERVES 6-8

Slice thin rounds from half of each of the orange, the lemon, and the lime. Squeeze the juice from the remaining halves to produce ¼ cup juice. Whisk the citrus juice, vinegar, oil, capers, garlic, celery salt, pepper flakes, and salt together in a bowl.

Bring a large pot of water to the boil. Add the shrimp to the water and cook for 3 minutes, then drain and place in a medium-sized bowl that will fit the shrimp snugly. Whisk the pickling liquid a few times and pour it immediately over the hot shrimp. The shrimp will not be cooked through, but will continue to "cook" in the acidic marinade. Add the sliced citrus fruits, bay leaves, and rosemary and stir to coat everything. Press the shrimp down to submerge it as much as possible in the pickling liquid. The citrus slices can rest on top. Place a piece of plastic wrap directly over the shrimp, then place a plate on top to keep the shrimp submerged in the marinade.

Cover the bowl and refrigerate at least overnight, but 3 days is better. Stir a couple of times a day. The shrimp will keep, covered in the fridge, for up to 2 weeks.

Shrimp with White and Red Remoulade

I think you can't go wrong with a lovely bowl of big shrimp on the buffet table. The pretty pink stripes add a nice dash of color, and the shrimp are always devoured. Tangy remoulade makes a great dip. I never can decide which version I prefer—white or red—so I include them both. Frankly, I usually serve them both.

SERVES 6–8, WITH ABOUT 2 CUPS OF EACH SAUCE

FOR THE WHITE REMOULADE

1 clove garlic

2 green onions, white and light green parts, roughly chopped

2 tablespoons flat-leaf parsley

1 cup mayonnaise, preferably Duke's

¼ cup Creole mustard (such as Zatarain's)

2 tablespoons white wine

1 tablespoon fresh lemon juice

1 tablespoon grated horseradish from a jar

½ teaspoon hot sauce (such as Crystal)

FOR THE RED REMOULADE

1 celery stalk, roughly chopped

1 clove garlic

2 tablespoons flat-leaf parsley

1 cup mayonnaise

½ cup Creole mustard (such as Zatarain's)

¼ cup ketchup

1 tablespoon grated horseradish from a jar

2 teaspoons celery salt

1 teaspoon sweet paprika

1 teaspoon hot sauce (such as Crystal)

FOR THE SHRIMP

5 cups water

1 cup white vinegar

1 lemon, halved

½ medium white onion

3 bay leaves

A handful of herbs— anything you have around, such as tarragon, dill, thyme, and parsley

2 pounds large shrimp, peeled and deveined

For the white remoulade, put the garlic, green onions, and parsley in the bowl of a small food processor or blender and pulse to finely chop. Scrape down the sides of the bowl, then add the remaining ingredients and blend until smooth and thoroughly combined. Pour the remoulade into a bowl, cover, and refrigerate for several hours, though this can be made 2 days ahead.

For the red remoulade, put the celery, garlic, and parsley in the bowl of a small food processor or blender and pulse to chop finely. Scrape down the sides of the bowl, then add the remaining ingredients and blend until smooth and thoroughly combined. Pour the remoulade into a bowl, cover, and refrigerate for several hours, though this can be made 2 days ahead.

For the shrimp, pour the water and vinegar into a large pot and add the lemon, onion, bay leaves, and herbs. Bring to a boil, then add the shrimp and cook until just pink, firm, and curled, about 3–4 minutes. Drain in a colander and immediately cover with ice to stop the cooking. Remove the onion, lemon, herbs, and bay leaves and discard.

The shrimp can be kept covered and chilled for 24 hours. Serve cold with the remoulades.

Smoked Catfish Spread

Catfish is so ubiquitous in the South, people are always looking for ways to serve it other than fried. Not that there is anything wrong with fried, but it's nice to push the boat out occasionally, so to speak. Sometimes I find smoked catfish at local grocery stores, but it's pretty easy to smoke it yourself. This spread wins rave reviews whenever I serve it.

MAKES ABOUT 2 CUPS

2 catfish fillets, boneless and skinless
8 ounces cream cheese, softened
1 cup sour cream
3 green onions, white and light green parts
2 teaspoons capers in brine
1 teaspoon fresh lemon juice
1 teaspoon Dijon mustard
½ teaspoon kosher salt
1 teaspoon freshly ground black pepper

First, smoke the catfish. There are several options here. You can use a big outdoor smoker contraption, a smoke box for your outdoor grill, a purpose-built stovetop smoker, or a homemade stovetop smoker. If you use one of those serious outdoor barbecue smokers, follow the manufacturer's instructions. For a grill smoke box or a stovetop smoker, bought or jerry-rigged (see the sidebar on page 74), lightly brush the fillets with oil and place on the cooking grates or surface. Smoke the fillets for 30–40 minutes until they are a dark caramel brown. (It may take longer on a large grill with a smoke box.)

When the fish has smoked and is warm enough to handle, flake it into a small bowl using a fork and your fingers, removing any stray bones or overly crisp end pieces. Leave to cool completely.

Place the flaked catfish, cream cheese, sour cream, green onions, capers, lemon juice, mustard, salt, and pepper in the food processor and process until smooth, but with a little texture to it. Scrape into a bowl and refrigerate for several hours or overnight to allow the flavors to meld.

Serve with melba toast or hearty crackers.

If you'd like to make this a bit fancier and call it catfish paté, use only ½ cup sour cream and pack it into bowl or terrine lined with plastic wrap. Refrigerate until firm, then invert onto a platter and remove the plastic wrap.

THE STOVE-TOP SMOKER

You will need:

1 (13 × 9-inch) deep disposable aluminum
    pan (often called a lasagna pan)
1 (13 × 9-inch) shallow disposable
    aluminum pan (often called a cake pan)
Heavy-duty aluminum foil
Wood smoker chips

When you are in the store purchasing your pans, make sure that the shallow pan fits inside the deeper pan without touching the bottom. A little gap around the edges of the pan is okay. If you find a shallow grill pan that already has holes in it, that will work perfectly (it should still fit inside the deep pan).

Using a knife or scissors, poke holes in the bottom of the shallow pan. You want plenty of holes so the smoke gets through. Line the bottom of your deep pan with a double layer of aluminum foil. Sprinkle about ½ cup of wood chips evenly over the bottom of the pan. Place the shallow pan on top of the deep pan and seal the pans together with aluminum foil. You want to create an airtight seal so that the smoke will not escape.

Brush the shallow dish lightly with oil and place the food to be smoked on top. Cover the whole affair with a couple of layers of aluminum foil, making sure again that there is an airtight seal all the way around. Some smoke will inevitably escape, but you want to keep as much in the smoker as possible.

Turn on your extractor fan and place the smoker over a stove burner on medium heat and smoke the food as recommended in the recipe. A nice, smoky smell will let you know it's working (it's like a wood fire, not an unpleasant smell), and small whiffs of smoke will appear. If you check on the progress, wear oven mitts and pull back just a corner of the foil, then make sure you seal it up tight again.

When the smoking process is completed, let everything cool completely and discard the pans and the foil.

TIPS
If you like this method and do it a lot, you can dedicate a real metal baking tray to be the bottom of your smoker. Once you've

smoked in it, you won't want to use it for anything else.

You can also use this setup on an outdoor gas grill.

The wood smoker chips you are looking for are practically sawdust. They are available at places that sell grills and smokers or online. The fine dust creates smoke quickly, which is important here because you can't really leave this makeshift smoker on the stove for more than about an hour without the bottom of the pan weakening.

This is not a method for slow-smoking ribs or ham that take hours, but it is great for adding smoke to quick-cooking foods without compromising the bottom of the pan.

I love to smoke shrimp this way, serving them with Comeback Sauce, or to smoke thin chicken breasts. One of my favorite uses for this technique is smoking halved plum tomatoes, then pressing them through a sieve to create a smoky tomato sauce.

Watermelon Rind Mignonette for Oysters

½ cup finely chopped
    pickled watermelon rind,
    from an 8-ounce jar
1 tablespoon finely minced
    shallot, about 1 small
    shallot
¼ cup rice vinegar
1 teaspoon pickling liquid
    from the watermelon
    rind jar
1 teaspoon fresh lime juice
1 teaspoon granulated sugar
Several grinds of black
    pepper

I owe this idea to food stylist Marian Cooper Cairns, who told me once that her best birthday party ever involved an oyster bar with a wide array of sauces, including a watermelon rind mignonette. She didn't have a recipe, but the idea intrigued me, so I worked out this one myself. The sweet and tangy pickled rind with the jazzy hit of vinegar and shallot perfectly complements briny oysters. Look out for watermelon rind pickles at your local farmers' market; commercial varieties are available at some grocery stores and gourmet markets. Rice vinegar is readily available and is a bit milder than a white wine version. I won't tell you how to shuck an oyster here—that's what Internet videos are for.

MAKES ABOUT 1 CUP

Make sure to chop the watermelon rind into very fine pieces, so it can be slurped up with the oysters. Combine all the ingredients in small bowl, cover, and refrigerate for several hours to let the flavors blend. Spoon over oysters on the half shell.

Petite Crawfish Pies

FOR THE CRUST

1 cup (2 sticks) unsalted
  butter, softened
8 ounces cream cheese,
  softened
2 cups all-purpose flour
½ teaspoon kosher salt

FOR THE FILLING

3 green onions, white and
  light green parts
2 celery stalks
1 green bell pepper, ribs
  and seeds removed
½ medium yellow onion
2 cloves garlic
¼ cup olive oil
12 ounces frozen crawfish
  tails, thawed, rinsed,
  and drained
½ cup plain dry bread
  crumbs
Kosher salt, to taste
Creole seasoning (such
  as Tony Chachere's)

I have experienced two versions of crawfish pie. My brother used to bring back a cooler full of crawfish pies from Louisiana business trips that were half-moon-shaped fried pies with a simple crawfish filling. But they are sometimes a little more pastry than crawfish. And many community cookbooks from Louisiana have recipes for a full pie—double crust with a creamy filling, sort of a crawfish pot pie. Not easy to eat as a snack. So, with a little ingenuity, I have combined the two, et voilà, Petite Crawfish Pies. Bite-size with a good pastry-to-filling ratio and an easy snack to serve and eat.

MAKES 36

For the crust, beat the butter and the cream cheese together in the bowl of a stand mixer with the paddle attachment until light and fluffy. Slowly beat in the flour and the salt until the dough comes together in a ball. Scrape down the sides of the bowl as needed. Knead the dough a few times to bring it all together, then gather it into a ball and wrap in plastic wrap. Refrigerate for 30 minutes to an hour.

For the filling, cut the green onions, celery, green peppers, and onions into chunks and place them in the bowl of a food processor. Add the garlic and pulse a number of times until you have a rough purée. You do not want a paste or to grind out a lot of liquid; the vegetables should be finely chopped but dry. Heat the olive oil in a large, deep skillet over medium-high heat, then add the vegetables and cook until they are pale and soft. Pulse the crawfish tails in the food processor—again you want them finely chopped, not paste. Add the crawfish to the skillet with the vegetables and stir to combine. Use a fork if needed to separate any clumps of vegetables or crawfish and to make sure everything is evenly distributed. Cook until the mixture is heated through, then add ½ cup water and cook until the liquid is almost completely evaporated, stirring constantly. Remove the pan from the heat and stir in the bread crumbs until they are evenly distributed and the filling is cohesive. Taste, and season with salt as needed. Leave to cool.

To assemble, lightly brush the inside of 36 mini-muffin cups with oil. Take the dough from the refrigerator and break off walnut-sized balls. Place a ball in each muffin cup and use your thumbs or the back of a measuring teaspoon to press the dough up the sides of the muffin cups, forming little cases for the filling.

Fill each pastry case with the crawfish, filling completely to the top. Sprinkle the tops of each pie with a dash of Creole seasoning. Bake the pies for 20–25 minutes, until the tops and the sides of the pies are golden and a little crisp. Serve warm.

The unbaked pies can be made up to a day ahead and kept covered in the refrigerator.

You will have some filling leftover. Mix it with a little cream and serve with pasta, or blend it with a little cream cheese and spread on crackers.

CRAWFISH BOIL

Several years ago, for a significant birthday, my sister-in-law and I decided to throw a surprise party for my brother. We tossed around a few ideas yet just kept saying it was a shame we couldn't have a crawfish boil, which he would truly love. His birthday is in early July, right after crawfish season ends. But two of his college friends, both natives of Louisiana, assured us it was okay. You see, they had all the gear—the outdoor burners, the giant pots, the long stirring batons—and I am convinced they were just dying to use their gadgets. My sister-in-law and I deferred to those we thought more expert on the subject, and one of the Louisiana boys ordered the crawfish from his "special source."

On the day of the party, I had set up tables and chairs, beer coolers, a grill for some boudin one of the boys had acquired, centerpieces, party favors, the whole thing. The FedEx truck arrived around 3 p.m. to deliver the crawfish, and as the driver was unloading the boxes—about fifty pounds of crawfish— I remarked that they sure did smell a little funny. He looked me straight in the eye and said, "Yeah, they SURE do," and I realized he'd been in that truck with that smell all day in the July heat. When the crawfish instigators arrived to set up their gear, they opened the Styrofoam boxes. Almost all the crawfish were dead, except a handful of live ones that skedaddled out of the box of death as fast as their claws could carry them. The guys kept saying everything would be fine, and they did try to pick out enough live ones to cook, but it was a lost cause.

We had a debate about what to do with the dead, rotting, smelly crawfish, and the boys decided to call another college friend—who had just purchased a brand-new pickup. Nobody wanted to put those boxes in their car. He arrived and loaded the crates into his truck. By this point, we were pretty close to guests arriving. I took the cash out of everyone's wallet and sent a college student we had hired for the party to Kentucky Fried Chicken with a handful of money and instructions to buy as much chicken as that cash allowed.

The guests arrived, and then my

brother, and he was surprised and delighted. But the menu of boudin from the grill, the corn, potatoes, and sausage boiled in the giant crawfish pots, and KFC served right from the bucket was a little hard to explain. Our crawfish cleanup friend showed up late, and we asked him what he'd done with the corpses. He told us he drove around to different dumpsters behind grocery stores, quickly tossing in a box and driving away, so he wouldn't get caught. Then he went through a drive-through carwash, but that proved to be inadequate, so he took his shiny new truck to one of those power-wash places and cleaned it out himself. He rushed home, hopped in the shower, changed clothes, and got back in the truck, but he couldn't stand it and went back in to shower again and wash his hair. On Monday morning, my sister-in-law called the crawfish place, irate, and told them that all the mudbugs had arrived dead. The fellow on the other end of the line drawled, "Yeah, we were wondering about those." She got her money back, and we've never let those two boys be in charge of a party again.

Cajun Popcorn (Fried Crawfish Tails)

1 pound crawfish tail meat, thawed if frozen

2 cups whole buttermilk

2 tablespoons hot sauce (such as Crystal)

1½ cups yellow cornmeal

⅔ cup all-purpose flour

2 teaspoons Creole seasoning (such as Tony Chachere's)

½ teaspoon kosher salt

½ teaspoon freshly ground black pepper

Vegetable oil for frying

This recipe may smack a little of fast-food drive-throughs or cheap themed restaurants, but hey, there is a reason these things make it onto menus. Eminently snackable, crispy, and with a little spice, these babies can be served up in a basket, and laissez les bon temps roulez! Serve on their own or with Remoulade Sauce (page 70) or Creamy Creole Dip (page 6).

SERVES 6–8

Rinse the crawfish tails and pat dry with paper towels. Place the crawfish in a large zip-top bag. Pour over the buttermilk and add the hot sauce. Squish everything around to blend and coat the catfish. Place the bag on a plate to catch any drips, then refrigerate for 30 minutes.

When ready to cook, line a rimmed baking sheet with paper towels and place a wire rack on top. Pour the crawfish into a colander and leave to drain for about 15 minutes. Pour 2 inches of oil into a deep, heavy pot and attach a candy thermometer. Heat over medium-high heat to 375°. Place the cornmeal, flour, Creole seasoning, salt, and pepper into a large zip-top plastic bag and shake to combine. Drop a handful of the crawfish into the coating and shake to coat each piece thoroughly. Drop the tails into the oil a piece at a time, being sure not to crowd the pan. Fry until the tails are browned and float to the top, about 2 minutes, then remove the pieces to the wire rack. Repeat with the remaining crawfish. You can keep the crawfish warm in a 225° oven for 15 minutes before serving if needed.

The Meat of the Matter

Beef Tenderloin with Blue Cheese Biscuits and Green Onion Butter

The king of the southern buffet table. Whether a fancy Christmas Eve party, ringing in the New Year, a wedding celebration, or a special gathering of favorite friends, the tenderloin reigns supreme, the pink slices carefully fanned out on the silver tray, surrounded by curly parsley, with a gravy boat of sauce and a basket of rolls. I cannot count the times I have enjoyed beef tenderloin at parties in my life. The most traditional combination is beef with horseradish sauce, homemade mustard, and little half-moon-shaped dinner rolls. But I like to switch things up and go the full southern, with biscuits for serving and a tangy green onion butter.

SERVES 12

For the beef, pat the tenderloin dry with paper towels and place it on a platter. Mix the salt and peppers together in small bowl, then rub the mixture all over every side of the meat. Place the meat in the fridge, uncovered, for at least an hour, but longer is better, up to 24 hours.

Take the tenderloin out of the fridge an hour before cooking. Preheat the oven to 500°. Place the meat in a roasting pan and cook for 20 minutes (that's 5 minutes per pound, if you need to adjust for size). Turn the oven off, but do not open the door. Leave the tenderloin in the oven for 2 hours. Put a sticky note on the oven door warning others not to open it!

Remove the tenderloin from the oven and let the meat rest for 15 minutes before slicing.

For the biscuits, preheat the oven to 425°. Mix the flour, baking powder, salt, baking soda, and pepper together in a large bowl using a fork. Cut the butter into small pieces and toss into the flour. Using your good clean hands or a pastry blender, rub the butter and flour together until you have a fine meal. Stir in the blue cheese until thoroughly combined. Add ¾ cup of the buttermilk and stir with a fork to combine. Now work the dough gently with your hands to bring it together in a nice, cohesive mass. Add more buttermilk as

FOR THE TENDERLOIN

1 (4-pound) beef tenderloin, trimmed and tied
2 tablespoons kosher salt
1 tablespoon freshly cracked black pepper
½ teaspoon white pepper

FOR THE BISCUITS (MAKES ABOUT 24)

2½ cups soft wheat flour (such as White Lily)
2 teaspoons baking powder
¾ teaspoon kosher salt
½ teaspoon baking soda
½ teaspoon freshly ground black pepper
⅔ cup unsalted butter, cold
¾ cup crumbled blue cheese
1 cup whole buttermilk, plus a little for brushing

FOR THE GREEN ONION BUTTER

6 green onions, white and light green parts only, chopped into small pieces
¼ cup parsley
1 cup (2 sticks) unsalted butter, room temperature
1 teaspoon kosher salt
2 teaspoons freshly ground black pepper

needed. Lightly flour a surface and dump the dough onto it. Turn the dough over once or twice to bring it together, then roll it out to ¼ inch thick with a lightly floured rolling pin. Cut the dough into 2-inch squares or with a 2-inch round cutter dipped in flour. Place the biscuits very close together—almost touching—on a rimmed baking sheet lined with parchment paper. Brush the tops with buttermilk. Bake for 8–10 minutes, until firm and lightly golden.

For the green onion butter, place the green onions and the parsley in the bowl of a food processor and pulse until very finely chopped, scraping down the sides of the bowl a couple of times. Add the butter, salt, and pepper and blend until smooth and well combined. Scrape the butter into a bowl, cover, and refrigerate for several hours or for up to 3 days. Bring the butter to room temperature so that it is spreadable before serving with the biscuits.

MIDNIGHT SNACK

Krystal Hamburgers opened in Chattanooga in 1932 and has since become something of a southern icon. Krystal's fame is built on its signature small, square burgers cooked with onions and steamed on fluffy buns. I am told they are very much like White Castle burgers, but I've never been to a White Castle. Krystal burgers are generally sold in bulk, each burger in its own little square box. In my wild and misspent youth, Krystal was the only purveyor of food open after midnight, except a few all-day coffee shops. So after a night on the town, a stop at Krystal was the logical end. Krystal always has special deals on large quantities of burgers, so a bag of burgers and some cheese fries was the rule for revelers. I once loaded into a small car with about eight people to hit Krystal after the Elvis Candlelight Vigil marking the anniversary of Elvis's death. People are devoted to Krystal, I think, more because of the memories of crazy nights than because of the food itself. When I was planning weddings, I went to a Krystal and picked up two hundred burgers late in the evening to serve to reception guests on silver trays. I myself took a bride and groom through the drive-through when I provided transportation to the hotel after their vintage getaway car wouldn't start.

Grilled Andouille Doubloons with Sweet Potato Mustard

So, maybe I'm going a little overboard with the cute here, but cut your sausage into slices and they look like Mardi Gras doubloons, the coins thrown from floats during parades. They are also perfect for dipping in a super-southern tangy mustard made with sweet potatoes.

SERVES 6–8, WITH ABOUT 1½ CUPS MUSTARD

In a saucepan over high heat, bring the vinegar to a boil. Remove from the heat and add the mustard seeds, bay leaf, and cinnamon stick, stirring to combine. Cover the saucepan and let the mixture rest at room temperature for about an hour. The seeds will absorb the liquid.

Remove the bay leaf and the cinnamon stick, scraping off any clinging seeds. Add the water, sorghum, and bourbon to the mustard seeds and stir, then scrape the mixture into the carafe of a blender. Blend until smooth, then add the sweet potato purée and blend until you have a cohesive, smooth paste. You can add a few drops of water as you go if you need to get things moving.

Pour the mixture back into the pan and heat over medium heat, bringing it to a boil. Reduce the heat to medium-low and continue to boil gently for approximately 5 minutes, stirring frequently to prevent scorching. Whisk in the sugar, dry mustard, paprika, and salt. Continue to simmer over medium-low heat, cooking the mixture until it has reduced a bit and is thick and spreadable, about 10 minutes.

Cool the mustard in the pan, then scrape it into an airtight container. The mustard will keep for about 2 weeks in the fridge.

Slice the andouille into coins about ¼ inch thick. Heat a grill pan over medium-high heat. Brush the slices with a little vegetable oil, then grill just until marked and warm through. Serve immediately with the sweet potato mustard for dipping.

½ cup apple cider vinegar
⅓ cup yellow mustard seeds
1 bay leaf
1 cinnamon stick
1 cup water
½ cup sweet potato purée (see Note)
1 tablespoon sorghum syrup or light molasses
1 tablespoon bourbon
¼ cup granulated sugar
2 tablespoons dry mustard
½ teaspoon sweet paprika
½ teaspoon kosher salt
1 pound andouille sausage
Vegetable oil

Note: To make things quicker, I happily use canned sweet potato purée, but only plain all-potato purée, not sweetened or seasoned. I find it at better markets and whole food stores. If you can't find it, wrap a sweet potato in foil, bake until soft (about 1 hour), and then blend the flesh with a little water to make a smooth purée.

Sweet Tea–Brined Pork Tenderloin with Sweet Tea Mustard

If beef tenderloin (see page 85) is the king of the southern buffet table, pork tenderloin is the queen. More economical and eminently adaptable, everyone will be satisfied with a hearty bite. A platter of thinly sliced pork surrounded by rolls with a bowl of sauce is another party staple. I've upped the southern factor with a happy hit of sweet tea, both in the marinade and in the zippy mustard sauce. And you'll find a host of other uses for the mustard.

SERVES AT LEAST 12, WITH 1 PINT MUSTARD

For the tenderloin, stir 2 cups of the water, the sugar, and the salt together in a saucepan. Bring to a boil, stirring to dissolve the sugar and salt. Remove from the heat and add the tea bags and the mint. Leave to cool, then remove the tea and the mint and stir in the remaining water. Place the pork tenderloins in a flat container or a zip-top bag placed on a plate. Pour the cooled brine over the tenderloins and refrigerate for 8 hours, but up to 12 is fine.

When ready to cook the pork, preheat the oven to 425°. Heat the olive oil in a large oven-proof skillet and brown the outside of the tenderloins on all sides. Transfer the skillet to the oven and cook the pork to an internal temperature of 150°, about 15 minutes. Let the pork rest at least 5 minutes before thinly slicing.

Serve thin slices of pork on a platter with the mustard and a basket of rolls.

For the mustard, pour the boiling water over the tea bag in a measuring jug and leave it to cool to room temperature. Set up a double boiler over medium-high heat.

Place the cooled tea and the remaining ingredients in the carafe of a blender and blend until smooth. Pour the mustard mixture into the top of the double boiler and cook, stirring, until the mustard thickens, about 8 minutes. You want it just a little looser than sandwich-spreadable; it will thicken as it cools and refrigerates. Cool the mustard in the pot off the heat, then pour it into a jar, cover, and refrigerate. The mustard will last a week tightly covered in the fridge. Bring to room temperature before serving.

FOR THE TENDERLOIN
- 4 cups water, divided
- ½ cup granulated sugar
- ½ cup kosher salt
- 4 black tea bags (such as orange pekoe)
- 4 sprigs fresh mint
- 2 pork tenderloins (about 2 pounds each)
- 2 tablespoons olive oil
- 2–3 dozen Parker House rolls (such as Sister Schubert's), prepared according to package instructions

FOR THE MUSTARD
- ½ cup boiling water
- 1 black tea bag (such as orange pekoe)
- 2 large eggs
- ¾ cup granulated sugar
- ½ cup white wine vinegar
- ½ cup ground mustard
- 1 teaspoon kosher salt
- ¼ teaspoon ground turmeric (optional, for color)

Natchitoches Meat Pies with Buttermilk Dip

I tend to be a restaurant loyalist. When I find a dish I really love, I order it at every visit. Such is the case with the Natchitoches meat pies at the Second Line here in Memphis. I order them every single time, no matter what else I, or anyone at the table, orders—and I am not very friendly about sharing. I only realized what an obsession it was when I arrived for a meal one time and chef-owner Kelly English asked me if I had come in for some meat pies. This version is my homage to Kelly's brilliant dish.

MAKES 18–20 MEAT PIES WITH 1 ½ CUPS DIP

FOR THE BUTTERMILK DIP
1 green onion, white and
    light green parts
½ cup whole buttermilk
½ cup mayonnaise,
    preferably Duke's
¼ cup sour cream
1 teaspoon Creole mustard
    (such as Zatarain's)
1 teaspoon hot sauce
    (such as Crystal)
A few grinds of black pepper

FOR THE PASTRY
2½ cups all-purpose flour
2 teaspoons kosher salt
½ cup vegetable oil
½ cup ice water

FOR THE FILLING
2 tablespoons (¼ stick)
    unsalted butter
½ pound ground beef chuck
½ pound ground pork
5 green onions, white and
    light green parts
¼ green bell pepper
1 clove garlic
1 tablespoon tomato paste
1 teaspoon kosher salt
¼ teaspoon ground thyme
¼ teaspoon cayenne pepper
¼ teaspoon ground cloves
⅛ teaspoon ground coriander
⅛ teaspoon ground nutmeg
Generous grinds of black
    pepper

FOR ASSEMBLY
1 large egg
2 tablespoons whole milk

For the dip, cut the green onions into small pieces and drop in the bowl of a food processor (I like a mini for this). Pulse a few times, then add the remaining ingredients and process until well blended. Transfer the dip to a bowl, cover, and refrigerate for several hours to allow the flavors to blend, but this can be made up to 4 days ahead.

For the pastry, place the flour and the salt in the bowl of a food processor and pulse a few times to combine. With the motor running, drizzle in the oil until the flour is wet and moistened. Stop and scrape down the sides of the bowl. Turn the motor on and drizzle in the ice water until the dough just comes together around the blade. You can use a bit more water if needed. Divide the dough in half and place each piece on a sheet of plastic wrap. Knead a little to make sure the dough all comes together, then pat each piece into a disk and wrap tightly. Refrigerate for at least 30 minutes, but a few hours is fine.

For the filling, melt the butter in a deep skillet, then break up the beef and pork into the pan. Cook the meat until it is no longer pink in the middle, breaking it into small pieces with a spatula or wooden spoon as you go. While the meat is cooking, chop the green onions into small pieces and drop them into the bowl of the cleaned-out food processor. Cut the bell pepper into pieces and add it to the processor with the garlic. Pulse a few times to chop everything finely; scrape down the side of the bowl and pulse until finely chopped. When the meat is browned, add the vegetables to the skillet and cook until they are soft and glassy, about 5 minutes. Stir in the tomato paste and cook for a few minutes, then sprinkle over the thyme, cayenne, cloves, coriander, nutmeg, and black pepper. Stir to combine and cook for a further 3 minutes or so, until the meat is fragrant. Remove from the heat to cool. When the filling has cooled, clean out the food processor bowl, then put the filling in it and pulse several times until the meat is finely chopped and the mixture holds together, a little like sausage.

To assemble, line a baking sheet with parchment paper.

Whisk the eggs and milk together until completely combined. Lightly flour a work surface. Unwrap 1 piece of dough and roll it out into a 12-inch round using a lightly floured rolling pin. Use a 3-inch biscuit cutter to cut out 8–10 rounds of dough. Working 1 at a time, place about 1 tablespoon of filling on the center of each round. Lightly brush the edges of each round with the egg wash, then fold the round in half, enclosing the filling. Pinch the edges to seal, then crimp them with the tines of a fork to make sure they are well sealed. Place the pies on the prepared baking sheet. You can reroll the dough scraps once, but the finished product may look a little shaggier. Repeat with the remaining dough rounds, then with the second disk of dough. At the point, the baking sheet can be covered with plastic wrap and the pies refrigerated for up to a day. If storing, cover the egg wash with plastic and keep it refrigerated as well. Whisk before using.

When ready to cook, preheat the oven to 350°. Lightly brush the top of each meat pie with the egg wash, then bake for 20–25 minutes, until golden brown and heated through. Serve hot or warm.

I frequently have some filling leftover, which is never a bad thing to me.

Chafing Dish Tamale Balls

FOR THE MEATBALLS

1 pound ground pork
1 pound ground beef
1 (14.5-ounce) can whole
    tomatoes
1½ cups yellow cornmeal
½ cup all-purpose flour
1 tablespoon chili powder
1 teaspoon kosher salt
½ teaspoon ground cumin
4 cloves garlic, finely
    minced
1 large egg

FOR THE SAUCE

1 (14.5-ounce) can diced
    tomatoes
1 (10-ounce) can mild diced
    tomatoes with green
    chiles (such as Ro-Tel)
1 tablespoon chili powder
1 teaspoon kosher salt

Hot tamales are the iconic dish of the Mississippi Delta. There is even a Hot Tamale Festival in Greenville every year that is a great deal of fun. The Southern Foodways Alliance has done research on the origins of tamales, and created documentaries and a "Tamale Trail" of places to eat. I love Delta tamales. I pick them up by the dozen when I am in Mississippi and keep a stash in the freezer. But I'll be honest, making real tamales is more work than I am willing to do—encasing the filling in the cornmeal dough, wrapping in corn husks. So this is my compromise, a party-perfect chafing dish extravaganza that really does mimic the original awfully well.

MAKES ABOUT 60

For the meatballs, place the ground beef and the ground pork in a large bowl and leave for about 30 minutes for the chill to come off. It is not pleasant working with fridge-cold meat.

Pour the can of tomatoes into the carafe of a blender and purée until smooth. Measure out ¾ cup tomato juice and leave the rest in the blender and set aside.

Line a baking sheet with waxed paper and set aside.

Add the cornmeal, flour, chili powder, salt, cumin, and garlic to the meat and use your good clean hands to begin mixing them together. When the meat is broken up and some of the cornmeal is mixed in, add ¾ cup of the remaining tomato juice and the egg and continue mixing and kneading until everything is thoroughly combined and cohesive. Begin to roll the meatballs in your hands, using about 1 tablespoon of meat for each ball. They will shrink slightly when cooking, but don't forget that people will be eating these off toothpicks, so don't go overboard. Place each meatball on the prepared baking sheet. When all the meatballs are rolled, place the baking sheet in the fridge for at least an hour to firm the meatballs, but at this point, you can freeze the meatballs on the sheet, then transfer to a zip-top bag and store for up to a week.

For the sauce, add the diced tomatoes and the tomatoes with green chiles to the tomato juice in the blender. Add the chili powder and the salt and purée until you have a smooth, thick sauce. This sauce can be refrigerated, covered, up to 3 days.

To assemble, when ready to serve, take the meatballs out of the fridge (thaw them in the fridge if they've been frozen). Pour 1 tablespoon olive oil in the base of a large, deep skillet or Dutch oven. Heat the oil over medium high, then brown the meatballs in the oil. You may need to do this in batches, setting the browned meatballs aside on a plate as you go. Just let the outside of the meatballs color; do not let them form a hard surface. Turn them to get as much of the meat browned as you can. When the meatballs are browned, pour in the sauce and return all the meatballs to the pan. Reduce the heat to medium and let the meatballs simmer and the sauce reduce for about 20 minutes. The meatballs must be cooked through with no pink in the center, and the sauce should be reduced so that it just coats the meatballs.

Transfer the hot meatballs and sauce to the vessel of a chafing dish to keep warm. Serve with toothpicks.

Sweet and Spicy Pecan Pepper Cocktail Bacon

2 pounds thick-cut smoked
   bacon
½ cup chopped pecans
½ cup light brown sugar
1 tablespoon all-purpose
   flour
½ teaspoon dry mustard
½ teaspoon freshly cracked
   black pepper
⅛ teaspoon cayenne
   pepper

One wedding reception venue in Memphis was known for its lacquered bacon bar snack. When I was planning weddings, people insisted that there be an endless supply of the shiny, sweet strips on every bar. Lines would form at these receptions as soon as guests arrived, not to greet the bride or the family, not to admire the flowers, not for the buffet, not even for drinks. Only for the bacon. It caused quite a scandal when a second, rival venue started offering the bacon as well, but there is no loyalty when it comes to lacquered bacon—the lines still formed. My favorite version is a little dressier than this standard, with crunchy pecans and snappy pepper. I list this recipe for two pounds of bacon, but I assure you, you can simply never have enough. Double or triple the amount, it will still be gone by party's end. Seriously. I made four pounds of this as a little snack for party for twenty people with a laden buffet, and they were gone before the ham biscuits came out of the oven.

MAKES 2 POUNDS

Preheat the oven to 375°.

Line 2 rimmed baking sheets thoroughly with foil. Place a wire rack in each baking sheet and spray with cooking spray. Place the bacon on the racks, close together but not touching.

Put the pecans, brown sugar, flour, mustard, black pepper, and cayenne in the bowl of a food processor fitted with the metal blade (I like to use a mini). Blend until the pecans are very finely chopped and everything is well combined.

Use a small spoon to sprinkle the pecan mixture carefully over each piece of bacon. Use the back of the spoon to spread the mixture in an even layer that completely covers the surface of the bacon. I find that I use about 2 teaspoons per piece. Press the filling firmly into each piece of bacon with the back of the spoon.

Place the baking sheets on two racks in the oven and set the timer for 15 minutes. At the end of the time, swap the baking sheets from the upper to the lower and the lower to the upper racks and cook the bacon for another 15 minutes. Check to see that the topping is brown and caramelized, but not burned. Cook for a further 5–10 minutes if needed, then remove from the oven to cool. You want the bacon a nice, dark brown. It will crisp as it cools. The bacon can be cooked up to 4 hours ahead of serving.

I find it best to cut the bacon strips in half or in thirds when they are fully cool, so that they are easy to pick up with one hand while you hold a glass of bourbon in the other.

Note: There is a product called baking paper, which is parchment on 1 side and foil on the other. It is heavy duty and fits a rimmed baking sheet fully. It is perfect for cooking bacon in the oven because it makes cleanup easy.

BARBECUE NACHOS AND OTHER USES FOR 'CUE

As a born-and-raised Memphis girl, my blood runs part barbecue sauce. So any exploration of southern foodways for me is likely to loop back around to barbecue. But with the finest barbecue to be had five minutes away in every direction, I have never seen the point of smoking my own pig. I don't have the equipment or the patience. I admire and applaud if you do, and I certainly recommend using your own creation for any of these ideas. When I need a barbecue fix, I head out to one of my favorite joints and buy some expertly smoked pork shoulder.

The pork shoulder sandwich is the traditional method of serving pulled or chopped shoulder, but many creative ways of have risen up over the years, from spaghetti to salad. Pick up a couple of pounds of your favorite pork shoulder and put together one of these snacks.

BARBECUE NACHOS

I used to work with a caterer when I was planning parties who insisted that he invented barbecue nachos and always got quite riled up talking about other restaurants who claimed to have invented it and "say so right there on the menu." He claimed to have proof, but I cannot verify its authenticity. His nachos were delicious, but so are the many other versions around town. The minor league ball park in Memphis sells a combo of barbecue nachos and a big beer that is a highlight of attending a game. There is a restaurant close to where I live, and I often order the barbecue nachos instead of a shoulder sammich. To make barbecue nachos, spread some corn tortilla chips on one or two baking trays and warm them slightly. Sprinkle the chips with your favorite barbecue rub. Layer the chips with pulled pork and generous drizzles of barbecue sauce, then cover the whole affair with melted cheese sauce. You can add some sliced pickled jalapeños if you are so inclined. Serve with lots of napkins.

BARBECUE SLIDERS

This is another favorite from my professional party-planning days. At elegant events, particularly wedding related, Memphians always want to serve some kind of barbecue, but it can be a bit messy and a little casual. So when the slider rose to popularity, these were a frequent request. Spread the bottom half of small slider buns with a thin layer of barbecue sauce. Add a generous but not dangerous spoonful of shredded or chopped pork shoulder and a little dollop of coleslaw and cover with the top bun. Secure with a toothpick if you want to. Remember not to overfill these, or the filling will fall out onto somebody's party dress or tuxedo and ruin their whole night. Pass the sliders on silver trays with plenty of monogrammed napkins.

BARBECUE PIZZA

Again there is much debate in Memphis about who invented the barbecue pizza and who serves the best version. It is said Elvis ate barbecue pizza, so what higher recommendation can there be? Roll out your favorite pizza crust until thin and spread generously with barbecue sauce. Cover the sauce with pulled pork and sprinkle over some shredded cheddar cheese (smoked cheddar is particularly nice). You can add some diced red onion or sautéed white onion. Cook as you would any pizza. For parties or larger gatherings, you can roll the crust into a large rectangle and cut it into small squares, or make smaller pizzas that can be cut into small triangle slices. Or make mini-pizzas that are one or two bites.

Barbecue Rillettes

Rillettes (REE-yets) is a rustic French pork spread. I imagine that traditionally it is made with all sorts of leftover scraps of meat to stretch the animal as far as it can go. And coating meat with layer of fat was a pre-refrigeration preserving method. I first had rillettes, not surprisingly, in France at a bistro as part of a charcuterie platter with lots of other bits of porky delight like saucisson sec, pork terrine, country pâté, and jambon. I adored it, but rather assumed it was a mysterious French preparation no mere mortal American could ever master. Then I saw a recipe using the slow cooker and it made perfect sense. The first time I made rillettes, following the recipe precisely, I thought the whole time that I could do a barbecue version mixing Memphis and France using my house barbecue rub. And I was right. This version is a delicious twist to serving classic pork shoulder. Those French rillettes were served in a little wire-bail ceramic crock, but I think a classic Mason jar is the perfect way to serve this southern version.

MAKES 4–5 CUPS

For the rub, whisk together all the spices.

For the rillettes, pat the pork shoulder dry. Sprinkle the spice rub on a plate and roll the pork shoulder in it. Make sure you thoroughly coat every surface, nook, and cranny of the meat. Place the pork on the plate in the refrigerator for at least 8 hours, but up to 24 is good.

When ready to cook, cut the pork into 1-inch cubes and place in the crock of a slow cooker. Add the lard, scooped into small chunks, the beer, garlic, and bay leaves. Give it a good stir to distribute everything evenly. Turn the slow cooker on high for an hour until the lard has melted, then reduce the heat to low and cook until the meat is falling-apart tender, 6–8 hours.

Use a slotted spoon to remove the pieces of meat to the bowl of a stand mixer. Strain the liquid left in the slow cooker through cheesecloth or a thin cotton tea towel into a large measuring jug or bowl. Use the paddle attachment of the mixer at low speed to

FOR THE RUB

2 tablespoons sweet paprika
1 teaspoon kosher salt
1 teaspoon celery salt
1 teaspoon freshly ground black pepper
½ teaspoon onion powder
½ teaspoon chili powder
½ teaspoon crushed red pepper flakes
½ teaspoon garlic powder
½ teaspoon smoked paprika
¼ teaspoon cayenne pepper

FOR THE RILLETTES

1 (3-pound) boneless pork shoulder
10 ounces lard
1 cup beer, lager or golden ale
5 cloves garlic
2 bay leaves

break the meat into strands. Chill the meat and the reserved liquid for 2 hours, or until the fat has solidified on the reserved cooking liquid.

Scoop the solidified fat off the cooking liquid and place it in a small pan over low heat to melt it. Return the meat to the mixer and beat on low again, adding some of the defatted cooking liquid until you have a creamy, spreadable paste.

Press the rillettes into ramekins or canning jars (about 6 half-pint), eliminating any gaps or air bubbles. Smooth the top of the rillettes. Pour a layer of the melted fat over the top of each container, making sure there is no meat poking through. Refrigerate until the fat has solidified, then cover. The rillettes may be stored in the fridge for a week or frozen for up to 3 months.

Serve at room temperature with crackers or toasted baguette slices. Scoop the knife down through the lovely layer of fat and spread away.

Because of the spices used, the rendered fat takes on a vibrant orange hue, rather than the pale yellowish white of traditional rillettes.

Kentucky Hot Brown Bites

The Kentucky hot brown sits high on the list of iconic southern sandwiches, originally served at Louisville's Brown Hotel. And rightfully so—hot, melty cheese sauce napped over turkey with a topping of bacon—what's not to love? So here's a party-perfect snack-size version that is always a hit. I find that the little 2-inch square party-size bread is available around holidays, but if you can't find it, cut very thin white sandwich bread into squares.

MAKES 24

Melt the butter in a saucepan, then whisk in the flour until smooth and pale. Whisk in the milk until the sauce is smooth and thickened, then whisk in the Dijon, salt, and pepper. Stir in the cheese until melted and smooth, then remove the pan from the heat and stir in the diced turkey and bacon. Leave the mixture to cool, then cover and refrigerate for up to 12 hours.

When ready to serve, preheat the oven to 350°. Lay the bread slices out on a baking sheet lined with parchment paper. Spread about 1 tablespoon of the mixture on each of the slices, then bake the bites for 10–15 minutes, until the topping is bubbling and melty.

I use about ½ pound of oven-roasted turkey sliced about ¼ inch thick, then diced into very small cubes. I ask the deli counter to slice the turkey on the thick side.

3 tablespoons unsalted butter

3 tablespoons all-purpose flour

1 cup whole milk

2 teaspoons Dijon mustard

1½ cups grated sharp white cheddar cheese

1½ cups finely diced cooked turkey

6 strips of bacon, cooked and diced

Kosher salt and freshly ground black pepper to taste

24 slices party-size white bread

Bama Wings with White Sauce

FOR THE SAUCE

1 cup mayonnaise,
    preferably Duke's
½ cup apple cider vinegar
1½ tablespoons freshly
    ground black pepper
1 tablespoon fresh lemon
    juice
1 teaspoon kosher salt
½ teaspoon hot sauce
    (such as Crystal)

FOR THE WINGS

24 chicken wings
3 cups whole buttermilk
1 tablespoon hot sauce
    (such as Crystal)
1 teaspoon kosher salt
½ teaspoon freshly ground
    black pepper
½ teaspoon smoked
    paprika

This sauce is called by some white barbecue sauce, a specialty of Alabama. But being a loyal Memphian of long standing, I find it hard to call anything but the barbecue sauce of my birthplace by that name. Nonetheless, it is a delicious accompaniment to chicken.

MAKES 24 WINGS AND ABOUT 1 ½ CUP SAUCE

For the white sauce, whisk all the ingredients together in a small bowl until thoroughly combined. Cover and refrigerate for several hours, up to 24, to allow the flavors to blend.

For the wings, place the wings in a large bowl or zip-top plastic bag and pour over the buttermilk and hot sauce. Stir to combine, making sure the wings are covered with the buttermilk. Leave in the fridge to marinate for at least 6 hours, but overnight is fine.

When ready to cook, preheat the oven to 400°. Line a rimmed baking sheet with foil, then place a wire rack on it. Spray with cooking spray. Remove the wings from the marinade and shake to remove any excess buttermilk. Place the wings on the prepared rack.

Mix the salt, pepper, and smoked paprika together in a small bowl. Sprinkle the spice mixture evenly over the wings. Bake the wings for 30–40 minutes. Pour about ½ cup of the white sauce into a small bowl, and brush a light coat over the wings and finish cooking until the internal temperature reaches 165°, about 10 more minutes. I like to set a probe thermometer for 150°, then brush the wings and continue cooking until I hit 165°. To avoid contamination, do not dip the basting brush into the white sauce that you will use as a dip—keep them separate!

Serve the wings hot with the remaining white sauce on the side for dipping.

OPENING DAY OF DOVE SEASON

Hunting is such a big part of southern culture that we even turn it into a party. The opening day of dove season falls on Labor Day weekend or thereabouts, when we like to think it's getting cooler outside (it's not). Dove hunting doesn't require much special equipment or subterfuge—no duck blinds or deer hides—so it's perfect for less intensive hunters. My brother explained that at a big hunt, some people shoot their limit in the first fifteen minutes and some use boxes and boxes of shells and never hit a thing. People with good dove fields invite friends, family, neighbors, even business colleagues and clients to opening-day festivities. After the actual hunting is done, tables are set up, tents are pitched, or pickup tailgates are put down. Coolers of beer and flasks of bourbon appear—and a spread of good, hearty eats.

OPENING DAY RECIPES

Bourbon-Spiked Caramelized Onion and Bacon Dip

Bacon Pecan Cheese Ball

Citrus Pickled Shrimp

Zucchini Cornbread Bites

Dilly Beans

Boiled Peanuts

Venison Bruschetta with Cumberland Gap Sauce

Cumberland sauce is a traditional British sauce made with red currant jelly and port and served with red meat. I took that idea and made it more Cumberland Gap than Duke of Cumberland with blackberry and bourbon. (The Cumberland Gap is the junction of Tennessee, Kentucky, and Virginia.)

SERVES 10–12

For the sauce, melt the blackberry preserves in the bourbon in a small saucepan over low heat. Whisk in the lemon zest, lime zest, ¼ cup of the combined citrus juice, and dry mustard. Raise the heat to medium and bring the sauce to a nice bubble and cook, stirring frequently, until slightly reduced, thick, and syrupy, about 5 minutes. The consistency will be that of simple syrup. Remove from the heat and leave to cool. The sauce will thicken on cooling to the consistency of jelly. You want to be able to dollop it onto the venison.

For the venison, mix the kosher salt and water together in a small saucepan and bring to a boil, making sure the salt is thoroughly dissolved. Remove from the heat, add the balsamic, Worcestershire, rosemary, and peppercorns, then cover the pan and leave to cool. When the brine is cool, stir in the buttermilk. Pour the marinade over the venison in a zip-top bag, place it on a plate or bowl, and refrigerate for 12–24 hours.

Heat a large cast-iron skillet over high heat and sear the venison on each side until browned. Continue cooking until you have reached the desired doneness, keeping in mind that venison is more tender cooked rare.

Slice the venison into thin pieces. Place a few slices of venison on a baguette slice and top with a small dollop of sauce. Serve warm or at room temperature.

FOR THE SAUCE
6 tablespoons blackberry preserves
6 tablespoons bourbon
Zest and juice of 1 lemon
Zest and juice of 1 lime
1 teaspoon dry mustard

FOR THE VENISON
¼ cup kosher salt
2 cups water
2 tablespoons balsamic vinegar
1 tablespoon Worcestershire sauce
2 sprigs fresh rosemary
1 teaspoon black peppercorns
2 cups whole buttermilk
1 pound venison tenderloin, trimmed of sinew and fat
Baguette slices

Cured Duck Breast with Persimmon Chutney

FOR THE DUCK

3 cleaned, boned duck
    breasts
1 orange
½ teaspoon juniper berries
½ teaspoon black
    peppercorns
1 bay leaf
2–3 cups kosher salt,
    divided

FOR THE CHUTNEY

4 Fuyu persimmons
½ cup diced yellow onion
⅓ cup apple cider vinegar
½ cup granulated sugar
½ teaspoon freshly grated
    ginger
¼ teaspoon brown mustard
    seeds
¼ teaspoon coriander
    seeds

Anyone with a bird hunter in their family or circle of friends has often faced the prospect of being inundated with game. I once asked my brother for two duck breasts, and he delivered a sack of about twenty in the dark of night while I slept when I could not turn it away. Curing duck breasts is a unique way of serving the abundance, and it always impresses guests when you make your own charcuterie (no matter how simple it actually is). The pretty persimmon chutney is the perfect foil for the salty duck—if you can find locally grown persimmons, by all means use them.

SERVES 10–12, WITH 1½ PINTS CHUTNEY

For the duck, rinse the duck and pat it dry. Peel 3 wide strips of zest from the orange, put them in a spice grinder or small food processor along with the juniper berries, peppercorns, bay leaf, and ¼ cup of the salt, and grind until the mixture is finely chopped and combined. Pour a thick layer of salt into the bottom of an earthenware dish that just holds the duck. Add the flavored salt and stir it around with your fingers. Press the duck breasts into the salt and roll them around, covering them completely. Lay them flat, making sure they are resting on a layer of salt and not touching the bottom of the dish. Cover the duck breasts completely with the remaining salt. You don't have to fill the dish with salt—just make sure no duck meat is exposed. Cover the top with plastic wrap, and then place a brick or a large can of tomatoes (on its side) or another heavy weight on top of the dish. Transfer to the refrigerator and leave to cure for 1 week.

After a week, unearth the duck breasts from their salty blanket and brush off as much salt as you can. Use paper towels to thoroughly clean off the salt cure. Thinly slice the duck and serve on slices of baguette topped with the chutney.

For the chutney, cut the green leafy stem out of the persimmons, then peel them with a vegetable peeler. Finely dice the persimmons and put them in a medium pan with the remaining ingredients. Stir well and bring the chutney to a boil over medium-high heat.

Reduce the heat to medium and simmer until the persimmons are soft and coated with a thick syrup. You want a spreadable consistency. When the fruit is soft, I like to mash it a bit with a sturdy spoon or give it a little whir with the immersion blender.

Spoon the chutney into jars and refrigerate for several days before use. The chutney will keep in the fridge for 2 weeks.

VIENNA SAUSAGES AND SALTINES

My father was from Earle, Arkansas, in the rural farmland of the Arkansas Delta. When he was a teenager, he had a summer job with the Soil Conservation Service mapping out how much farmland was planted with cotton. The work was tedious and in the heat of a southern summer, and the vehicles were not air-conditioned. But he really explored the country and got to know many farmers and local communities. He and his companions had a lot of ground to cover each day, so lunch came from whatever little commissary or store they happened to be near. If he knew the store, they'd make him a sandwich, but as that was not often the case, he would buy a packet of saltine crackers and a can of Vienna sausages. When I asked him what he thought of when he thought of "Southern Snacks," his quick-as-lightning answer was a can of Vienna sausages and saltines.

HAM DUST

I was born and raised in Memphis, in western Tennessee, at the apex of the Mississippi Delta, home of fried catfish and fluffy buttermilk biscuits. But I have deep roots in the middle of the state as well. My mother is from Columbia, just south of Nashville. Columbia is home to the annual Mule Day parade, held the first weekend of every April. It's one of those timeless southern festivals, with agricultural contests, pageant queens, and performers, all focused around the magnificent mule. Perhaps this sounds familiar? Some years ago it was featured on the front page of the *New York Times*, above the fold, with a big color picture. It was part of a story on homeland security funding, as the festival has been listed as a top U.S. terror target. Maybe Mr. Bin Laden had use for mules in his Afghani mountain trekking at the time. But I'm no defense expert.

I remember Mule Day as a child. We had the advantage of watching the festivities from the window of my grandfather's law office on the town square. In Columbia, Mule Day was a chance to welcome visiting family members back home for the festivities. My grandmother and her friends took advantage of this opportunity to show off grandchildren from far-off places. Sort of their own Mule Queen Pageant of Progeny. At these rather elegant gatherings, also held at Christmas, Thanksgiving, and over summer vacations, the said grandchildren were cleaned and brushed and buttoned into their best sailor suits or smocked batiste dresses to be displayed to best advantage. Gracious hostesses opened their grand homes for afternoon gatherings or after-church lunches, tables laid with the finest linens and silver, freshly cut magnolia blossoms floating in an antique terrine at the center of it all.

In Middle Tennessee, the culinary feature was the country ham, a deeply smoked, salty slab of pig hung to smoke and cure for months. To be eaten, the hams had to be soaked in changes of water using a "ham stand," basically a large, steel lidded bucket designed to fit the whole ham and gallons of water. The ham was then scrubbed and cooked for hours, sometimes glazed in brown sugar, sometimes Coca-Cola (Co'cola, that is), sometimes with no embellishment at all. Then the great masterpiece was presented on a fine silver tray surrounded by curly parsley. The ham was sliced as best as possible; the dry, dense, rich, intensely salty meat fell off in slivers more often than not. And of course, the only true and proper accompaniment to real country ham is beaten biscuits, a lost culinary art. These little inch-round pucks are hard and flaky and crispy all at once.

Few people make beaten biscuits anymore, as the laborious process involves beating the kneaded dough with a bat or thwapping it on a wooden countertop until the dough blisters, then running the mass through a biscuit brake, a device that looks like an instrument of torture but rolls the dough to an elastic, smooth sheet. The biscuits are then cut, precisely pricked with a fork, and baked until dry. When ready to eat, these magnificent biscuits may look like hard tack, but the slight twist of a butter knife splits the biscuit perfectly, ready to receive a knob of butter and a slice of divine country ham.

In the evening, when the iced tea punch is gone, the cold fried chicken and stuffed eggs have been polished off, and the chess pies and caramel cakes are finished, the real treat comes. Ham dust. Ham dust is the shavings and scrapings left on the tray after the arduous process of dismantling the ham, when any whole slices have been wrapped in foil for another day and the bone has been set aside for black-eyed peas. This delicious detritus of a true country ham is swept into a bowl, mixed with the country butter, still soft from the table, and spread onto beaten biscuits. Of course, the irresistible beaten biscuits may not make it to the end of the party, but ham butter on soft slices of soft Bunny brand bread or saltine crackers are just as heavenly.

Mustard Poppy Seed Ham Rolls

1 large shallot

1¼ cups (2½ sticks) unsalted butter, room temperature

1 tablespoon Dijon mustard

1 tablespoon poppy seeds

1 teaspoon dry mustard

½ teaspoon kosher salt (omit if using country ham)

2 dozen Parker House rolls (such as Sister Schubert's), thawed

½ pound thinly shaved smoked city ham or country ham

1 tablespoon light brown sugar

I adore these. For years, I have volunteered to organize a Christmas potluck for one of my book clubs, solely so I could volunteer to bring these. They are cheesy and melty and buttery and just downright delicious.

MAKES 24

Cut the shallot into small pieces and place in the bowl of a food processor fitted with the metal blade (a mini is fine). Pulse to chop the shallots finely, then add the butter, cut into small pieces, the Dijon, poppy seeds, dry mustard, and salt. Blend until smooth and evenly combined. Scoop the butter mixture into a bowl, cover, and refrigerate for several hours to allow the flavor to blend, or up to 2 days ahead.

Bring the poppy seed butter to room temperature so it is easily spreadable. Scoop about 4 tablespoons of the butter into a small saucepan and set aside. Remove the entire round of rolls from each pan and use a long, sharp bread knife to slice each package of rolls in half horizontally. Do not separate the individual rolls: slice open the whole round. Spread the butter in an even layer over each of the bottom halves. Spread evenly to the edges of the bread. Carefully transfer the covered half of the rolls back to the pan they came in (or a similar pan). Divide the ham between the roll pans and layer it evenly over the poppy seed butter. Place the top halves of the roll over the ham. Use a thin knife to run through the separations in the rolls to make them easier to pull apart when cooked.

Add the brown sugar to the reserved butter in the saucepan and heat over medium, stirring, just until the sugar is dissolved. Pour half of the melted butter over each pan of rolls. Leave to cool and cover each pan tightly with foil. The rolls can be refrigerated for several hours at this point.

When ready to bake, preheat the oven to 350°. Bake the rolls, covered, for 30 minutes or until warmed through and golden. Serve immediately.

The Garden Path

Party Tomato Pies

No summer in the South would be complete without tomato pie: fresh-from-the-garden tomatoes layered in a pastry crust blanketed in mayonnaise and cheese. I mean, what's not to love? I just had to put together a perfect party version of the classic, and it is every bit as wonderful. Don't skimp on the basil.

MAKES 36

For the crust, beat the butter and the cream cheese together in the bowl of a stand mixer with the paddle attachment until light and fluffy. Slowly beat in the flour and the salt until the dough forms a ball. Scrape down the sides of the bowl as needed. Knead the dough a few times, then form it into a ball and wrap in plastic wrap. Refrigerate for 30 minutes to an hour.

For the filling, while the crust dough is chilling, cut the tomatoes in half and scoop out the seeds and pulp. Finely chop and place them in a colander. Sprinkle over the salt and toss to combine. Leave the tomatoes to drain for about an hour.

Mix the mayonnaise, cheese, basil, and pepper in a bowl, making sure the cheese is well blended with the mayo and there are no clumps.

To assemble, preheat the oven to 400°.

Lightly brush the inside of 36 miniature muffin cups with oil. Take the dough from the refrigerator and break off walnut-sized balls. Place a ball in each muffin cup and use your thumbs or the back of a measuring teaspoon to press the dough up the sides of the muffin cups, forming little shells for the filling.

Use a fork to fill each pastry cup with the tomatoes (a fork prevents too much liquid from getting into the crusts). Fill almost to the top of each crust. Spoon about a teaspoon of the mayo mix over the top of the tomatoes and spread to cover.

Place the muffin pans on a cookie sheet. A little oil will separate from the mayo while baking, and it can make a mess if it drips on the bottom of the oven. Bake the pies for about 20 minutes, until golden brown and bubbly on top. Let the pies rest for at

FOR THE CRUST
1 cup (2 sticks) unsalted butter, softened
8 ounces cream cheese, softened
2 cups all-purpose flour
½ teaspoon kosher salt

FOR THE FILLING
4 plum tomatoes
1 teaspoon kosher salt
1 cup mayonnaise, preferably Duke's
1 cup grated sharp cheddar cheese
3 tablespoons finely minced fresh basil
Generous grinds of black pepper

least 15 minutes before gently loosening them from the tins with a knife and transferring them to a plate. Serve warm or at room temperature.

The pies can be made a few hours ahead and baked, then kept in a covered container in the fridge. Place the pies on a baking sheet and warm in a 225° oven for a few minutes before serving. The pies can also be frozen. Place cooled pies on a baking sheet and freeze until firm, about an hour. Transfer to a rigid container and freeze for up to a month. Thaw in the fridge overnight, then transfer to a baking sheet and warm in a low oven.

KOOLICKLES

Drive through the Mississippi Delta, and the whole world is laid before you. Miles and miles of unbroken views. Acres of fields—cotton, soybean, some corn, some wheat, some rice. Green and brown and blue. You see the weather coming for miles. Driving through sun, but the thunderhead and the rain it is producing are visible just down the road, or miles and miles away—it's hard to tell. Drive through little towns, some with once-beautiful squares, some revamped and revitalized with boutiques and restaurants. Some just a few trailers, a couple of shotgun cabins, a post office, and a grocery. Stop at one of these markets or one of the small gas stations along Highway 61, and there on the counter is the brightest color you are likely to see in the Delta. A glowing neon jar of Koolickles.

Koolickles are pickles brined with Kool-Aid. How this came about, I cannot imagine and don't particularly want to know. Take the pickles out of a jar, add one of those small packets of Kool-Aid and a cup or so of sugar to the brine, then poke holes in the pickles and return them to the liquid and let them sit. Cherry is the most common flavor, producing an electric red, but any color of Kool-Aid will do, and you may well see a rainbow of flavors on offer.

Cherry Tomatoes with Creamy Buttermilk Dip

¾ cup whole buttermilk

½ cup mayonnaise, preferably Duke's

¼ cup sour cream

1 tablespoon chopped fresh chives

1 tablespoon chopped parsley

1 clove garlic, finely minced

Generous grinds of black pepper

Kosher salt to taste

4 pints cherry tomatoes, rinsed and dried

Sweet cherry tomatoes are wonderful little snack bites, and they grow like gangbusters in a southern garden—even my brown thumb can produce them. Pile up a platter or bowl with different colors and shapes of lovely small tomatoes and serve a bowl of luscious, creamy southern buttermilk dip alongside. As always, look out for a good, thick, and tangy local buttermilk.

MAKES ABOUT 1½ CUPS DIP

For the dip, whisk the buttermilk, mayonnaise, and sour cream together until smooth. Add the herbs and garlic and stir to combine. Stir in a generous amount on black pepper, then add salt to taste. Cover the dip and refrigerate for several hours or up to a day.

Serve with the cherry tomatoes.

The Soggy Tomato Sandwich

Sunday after-church lunches at my grandmother's generally included fried chicken or sometimes country ham, stuffed eggs, and tomato sandwiches. These were always described as soggy tomato sandwiches, because they are just perfect when the mayonnaise and the juice from the tomatoes begin to permeate the soft white bread. My dear sweet sister-in-law and I were once charged with making the tomato sandwiches at a family gathering at my aunt's house. We were slicing and spreading and chatting and maybe not paying as much attention as we should have. My aunt stopped my sister-in-law cold, chiding her for not getting the mayonnaise to the EDGE OF THE BREAD. After fourteen years of marriage, my sister-in-law thought she just might be expelled from the family. The tomato sandwich is such an important family legacy that when my mother read the manuscript for this book, she left three sticky notes with more instructions and reemphasizing the need to spread the mayonnaise to the EDGE OF THE BREAD.

Ripe summer tomatoes
Kosher salt and freshly ground black pepper
½ small white onion
Mayonnaise (highest quality, such as Duke's, or homemade)
Thinly sliced white sandwich bread

Slice the tomatoes—not too thinly. Lay the slices out on paper towels and sprinkle liberally with salt and pepper. Leave for at least 30 minutes (or while you go to church services). Cut the bread into rounds the size of the tomato slices with a biscuit cutter or glass. Spread each slice of bread with mayonnaise to the EDGE OF THE BREAD. Place a slice of tomato on a bread round. With a microplane or very fine grater, grate the onion over the tomato. Top with another bread round. Squash down lightly. Cover with damp paper towels until ready to serve.

FESTIVAL OF FOOD

I started this book asserting that southerners like to eat. But we also like to celebrate our food in unique and, well, interesting ways. Sure, there are now high-dollar food and wine festivals in all the culinary capitals of the South, featuring top-notch chefs, major national sponsors, TV coverage, and upscale beverages. But there is simply nothing like a small-town showcase of locally loved specialties. Cooking contests, eating contests, pageants, a crowned queen, and a parade, the whole community participating, family returning home for the event, and lots of visitors from out of town—all stops are pulled out.

Greenville, Mississippi, hosts the Delta Hot Tamale Festival every year, featuring a Miss Hot Tamale contest, in which the contestants must fashion outfits from corn husks, while the Kumquat Festival in Dade City, Florida, crowns both a Miss and a Mister Kumquat. The Gueydan, Louisiana, Duck Festival has categories for all ages,

including the Ti Tiny Queen (0–6 months), Tinincy Queen (24–36 months), and the more mature La Petite Queen (5–6 years). Luling, Texas, stages the Watermelon Thump every year, which obviously includes a seed-spitting contest, while eager contestants turn out for the Rotary Tiller Race at the Purple Hull Pea festival in Emerson, Arkansas (where you will also find roving Tiller Girls). Enter the sweet potato pie-eating contest at the Sweet Potato Festival in Vardaman, Mississippi, or try your luck at the cornbread eating contest at Columbia's South Carolina Cornbread Festival. If you are bold, don't miss the onion eating contest at the Vidalia Onion Fest in Georgia or ramp eating at the Whitetop, Virginia, Ramp Festival. Try your hand at the tomato packing contest at the Pink Tomato Festival in Warren, Arkansas, or the World-Famous Rolling in the Grits contest at the Grits Festival in St. George, South Carolina (yes, people roll around in a big vat of grits). The World Chicken Festival in Kentucky showcases the world's largest skillet, while the Georgia Peach Festival bakes up the world's largest peach cobbler, or visit the Word's Biggest Fish Fry in Paris, Tennessee. Stroll the Puddin' Path at the Banana Pudding Festival in Centerville, Tennessee, or Biscuit Boulevard at the International Biscuit Festival in Knoxville.

Seriously, all culinary bases are covered—Slugburgers in Corinth, Mississippi, RC Cola and Moon Pies in Bell Buckle, Tennessee, mullet in Swansboro, North Carolina, catfish in Belzoni, Mississippi, collards in Ayden, North Carolina, doodle soup in Bradford, Tennessee, burgoo in Lawrenceburg, Kentucky, shrimp and grits in Jekyll Island, Georgia, okra in Burkville, Alabama, boiled peanuts in Bluffton, South Carolina, sorghum in Blairsville, Georgia, pecans in Florence, South Carolina, oysters in Urbanna, Virginia. . . . See what I mean?

Watermelon with Country Ham and Watermelon Gastrique

1 small seedless
  watermelon, with 1 cup
  cut into chunks
1 cup white vinegar
2 cups granulated sugar
½ pound paper-thin country
  ham slices

I've always thought that the classic Italian dish of melon, usually cantaloupe, draped in salty prosciutto is one of those effortlessly elegant plates I aspire to flawlessly serve. I had to southern it up with our own gorgeous summer watermelons and fabulously salty country ham, sliced paper-thin. Sometimes the Italian version is served with a drizzle of balsamic vinegar, and in that spirit I created a vinegary melon syrup for drizzling. Look for country ham at the deli counter and ask that it be sliced paper-thin like prosciutto.

MAKES ABOUT 1 CUP GASTRIQUE

Purée 1 cup of watermelon chunks in a blender until smooth. Pour through a strainer into a large, high-sided saucepan. Stir in the vinegar and the sugar and bring to a low boil over medium-high heat. Watch carefully so it doesn't boil over—it makes a mess if it gets on the stove. Reduce the heat to a simmer and cook until reduced by more than half and thickened to the consistency of maple syrup. This could take as long as an hour. You want the syrup pourable, and it will thicken on cooling. Remove from the heat and leave to cool. Transfer to a jar and cover tightly. The gastrique will keep in the fridge for up to a month, so you'll have it ready to use each time you find a great summer watermelon. Warm it in a saucepan to loosen it up if needed.

There are many ways to serve this lovely dish: slice the watermelon into thin wedges and layer on a salad plate, draped with country ham and drizzled with gastrique, cut the watermelon into cubes, wrap them in the ham, skewer with a toothpick, and drizzle, or wrap long spears in the ham and brush gastrique over the surface.

Squash Pancakes with Pimento Pepper Relish

I think these little bites are rustic and elegant all at once. Full of fresh summer flavor, they have the look of the fancy blinis served with caviar. I top them here with a sweet and tangy relish made from pimentos. Because pimentos are for more than cheese.

MAKES ABOUT 20 SMALL PANCAKES AND 2 CUPS RELISH

For the relish, heat the oil in a large saucepan over medium heat, then add the drained pimentos. Cook, stirring frequently, until the pimentos soften slightly, about 3 minutes. Add the onions and cook, stirring frequently, until the onions are soft and glassy, about 5 minutes. Add the minced garlic and cook 1 minute more, then add the water and cook until the liquid has evaporated. Stir occasionally to prevent scorching. Stir in the vinegar, sugar, and paprika until well combined. Cook until the liquid is evaporated, again stirring to prevent the relish from catching on the pan. Remove from the heat and cool to room temperature. The relish can be cooled, covered, and refrigerated for up to 2 days.

For the pancakes, grate the squash onto a cotton tea towel with the large holes of a box grater. Leave on the counter for about 10 minutes, then twist the squash shreds in the towel to ring out as much liquid as possible. Leave to drain in a colander while you proceed. Beat the eggs in a bowl, then stir in the flour, baking powder, salt, and pepper until completely combined. Fold in the Parmesan, green onions, and chives until evenly distributed. Stir in the grated squash until it is fully incorporated.

Heat a few tablespoons of the olive oil in a large skillet over medium-high heat until shimmering. Scoop tablespoons full of the batter into the skillet and flatten with the back of a spatula. I like to use a 1 tablespoon cookie scoop. Do not crowd the pan; leave room for flipping. Cook until golden brown on the bottom side, about 3 minutes, then flip and cook until the other side is brown, about 2 minutes. Remove to a plate lined with paper towels to drain and repeat with the rest of the batter. Add more olive oil as needed.

Serve warm with a spoonful of the pimento pepper relish.

FOR THE RELISH

3 tablespoons olive oil
4 (7-ounce) jars diced pimentos, rinsed and drained
1½ cups finely chopped onion
1 clove garlic, finely minced
½ cup water
¼ cup apple cider vinegar
¼ cup granulated sugar
1 teaspoon sweet paprika

FOR THE PANCAKES

1 medium yellow squash
2 large eggs
¼ cup all-purpose flour
1 teaspoon baking powder
1 teaspoon kosher salt
½ teaspoon freshly ground black pepper
½ cup grated Parmesan cheese
3 green onions, light and white green parts, finely diced
1 tablespoon finely chopped chives
About ½ cup olive oil

Dilly Beans

¾ pound fresh green beans (enough to fill a quart jar)
2 cloves garlic, peeled
4–5 sprigs fresh dill
2 cups apple cider vinegar
2 cups water
4 tablespoons canning salt or 3 tablespoons table salt
1 tablespoon granulated sugar
½ teaspoon mustard seeds
½ teaspoon dill seeds

Putting things up is a time-honored southern practice that has come back into vogue. Once a necessity to provide food for the long winter months, canning is now a popular hobby from rural farms to urban lofts. I am a summertime canning obsessive, so all my cheese platters include the fruits (and vegetables) of my canning labors. And the relish tray has always been a popular addition to the southern table, with pickled green beans a favorite. In this simplified recipe, no canning is required. These quick pickles are delicious to eat out of hand but also make a spectacular garnish for a Bloody Mary.

MAKES 1 QUART OR 2 PINT JARS

Trim the ends off the beans, making sure they are a length to stand in the jar. Blanch the beans in boiling water for 2 minutes, then drain and cover with ice cubes to stop the cooking. Toss the ice around to get to all the beans. Drain.

Clean a 1-quart jar with a 2-piece lid. Stack the beans, garlic, and dill sprigs in the jar. I find it easiest to do this with the jar on its side, so that the beans stack on top of each other and stay upright.

Bring the vinegar, water, salt, sugar, and seeds to a full rolling boil and boil for 2 minutes. Carefully pour the liquid over the beans in the jar to cover, leaving ¼ inch headspace at the top. Immediately put on the top and screw on the band. Leave to cool 8 hours or so, then refrigerate for up to 2 weeks. There may be more pickling liquid than you need; save it in the fridge for your next batch or discard.

Note: Old-fashioned versions of this pickle always look so pretty with full heads of dill tucked inside, so if you have dill growing or a place where you can buy full dill seed heads, use about 3 of those with 1 dill sprig.

Zucchini Cornbread Bites

1 medium zucchini

1½ teaspoons kosher salt, divided

1½ cups all-purpose floor

¾ cups yellow cornmeal

1 tablespoon baking powder

¼ teaspoon freshly ground black pepper

¼ teaspoon cayenne pepper

1 cup whole buttermilk

2 large eggs

¼ cup (½ stick) unsalted butter, melted and cooled

1 tablespoon honey

1 cup finely grated cheddar cheese

Little mini-muffins are for more than breakfast—they make a great savory snack as well. Easy to make, easy to serve, and easy to eat.

MAKES 24

Preheat the oven to 350°. Spray 24 mini-muffin cups with cooking spray.

Grate the zucchini on the fine holes of a box grater onto a thin cotton tea towel. Sprinkle with 1 teaspoon of the salt and toss to combine. Leave to sit in the sink for about 10 minutes. Twist the zucchini in the tea towel to ring out as much liquid as you can.

Mix the flour, cornmeal, baking soda, remaining salt, black pepper, and cayenne together in a large mixing bowl. Make a well in the center of the dry ingredients and add the buttermilk, eggs, melted butter, and honey. Stir until the dry ingredients are moistened, then add the cheddar cheese and the grated zucchini. Use a fork to separate the zucchini strands and stir the muffins. Stir until combined and the cheese and zucchini are evenly distributed, with no dry ingredients visible in the bowl.

Fill the prepared muffin cups to the top with the batter. Bake until firm and a tester inserted in the center comes out clean, 12–15 minutes. Cool in the pan, then remove the muffins. The muffins can be stored in an airtight container for a day.

Note: Fill the muffin tins to the top and get a nice 2-bite, puffed-top muffin. If you'd like, you can fill the muffin cups ¾ full, reduce the cooking time, and bake 30 muffins that are a single-bite treat.

Green Beans with Creamy Bacon Vinaigrette Dip

The summer farmers' markets around here are awash in green beans, big bins piled high with all sorts of varieties. Crisp, fresh green beans make a wonderful dipper and a beautiful vegetable platter. A combination of green, yellow wax, and purple beans creates a stunning display (blanch the purple beans separately and only for a few seconds, as they lose their color quickly). This creamy bacon vinaigrette has smoky richness from the bacon grease and a good vinegary punch that complements the crisp beans. As a bonus, you get cooked bacon to snack on.

SERVES 10–12, WITH 2 CUPS DIP

Bring a large pot of water to the boil. While the water is heating, fill a sink or large bowl with ice and water. When the water has come to the boil, drop in the green beans and blanch for 1 minute, just until they turn bright green. Immediately drain the beans and drop them in the ice water to stop the cooking. Stir the beans around so they are all submerged in the ice water. When the beans are completely cool, drain and spread out on tea towels to dry. The beans can be blanched and stored in zip-top bags in the refrigerator for a day.

Place the remaining ingredients in the carafe of a blender and blend briefly until smooth. Do not overblend, or the cream will turn into butter. Check the seasoning and add more salt and pepper if you want. Pour the dressing into a jar, screw on the lid, and refrigerate for up to 3 days. Shake well to combine before serving.

Serve the dip surrounded by the chilled green beans.

The vinaigrette is a great dip for any vegetable and a rich dressing for a green salad.

2 pounds fresh green beans, tops and tails removed
3 tablespoons bacon grease (from about 8 strips of bacon), not solidified
¾ cup heavy cream
4 tablespoons white wine vinegar
6 tablespoons water
2 cloves garlic, minced
4 green onions, white and light green parts, cut into pieces
½ teaspoon kosher salt
Generous grinds of black pepper

Asparagus with Lemon Chiffon Sauce

1 large shallot, diced

1 clove garlic, minced

Leaves from 2 rosemary
stems

½ cup fresh lemon juice

1 cup white wine

⅓ cup heavy cream

6 tablespoons (¾ stick)
unsalted butter

3 pounds slim, tender
asparagus

Delicate spears of asparagus served with a creamy sauce have always been a staple of the southern buffet. It just looks so pretty, and it is simple to make and can be prepared ahead, so what's not to love? The dip is wonderful on any spring vegetable.

SERVES 10–12, WITH ABOUT ½ CUP DIP

Place the shallots, garlic, and rosemary in a saucepan and add the lemon juice and wine. Give them a good stir, then bring to a boil over medium-high heat. Boil gently until the liquid is reduced to ½ cup. Stir in the heavy cream and cook until the liquid is reduced a bit more and the sauce is thickened.

Place a fine-mesh strainer over a bowl or measuring jug and pour the sauce through, pressing on the solids to extract as much liquid as possible. Wipe out the pan and return the sauce to it. Place over low heat and whisk in the butter ½ tablespoon at a time, letting each piece melt before adding more. Transfer to a small bowl and let it come to room temperature. The sauce can be made a day ahead, cooled, covered, and refrigerated.

Snap off any woody ends on the asparagus and cut the stalks into even lengths. Fill a bowl with ice water and place it in a sink. Bring a large pot of water to a boil and drop in the asparagus (in batches if necessary). Blanch for 2–3 minutes, just until the bright green color comes out, then lift out the spears with tongs and drop them in the cold water to stop the cooking. Drain the asparagus through a colander as soon as it is cooled. Pat the asparagus dry with paper towels.

The asparagus can be prepared a day ahead and stored in the fridge in a zip-top plastic bag.

Overnight Onions

I went searching online some years ago for recipes to accompany a big family burger cookout, and I came across one similar to this. On the night, the onions were getting raves and my mom pointed out that her recipe for marinated onions appears in a Memphis Symphony League cookbook—but she'd never made them for me. I changed it up a little just to spite her!

MAKES ABOUT 4 CUPS

3 large Vidalia or sweet yellow onions
2 cups water
1 cup granulated sugar
½ cup white vinegar
½ cup mayonnaise, preferably Duke's
1 teaspoon celery seed
1 teaspoon celery salt
Dash of sweet paprika

Chop the onions into small pieces, easy to scoop onto a cracker, and transfer to a large bowl. Combine the water, sugar, and vinegar in a saucepan and bring to a boil, then pour the mixture over the onions. Cover and refrigerate overnight.

The next day, drain the onions completely, then stir in the mayonnaise, celery seed, celery salt, and paprika until well combined and all the onions are coated with mayo. Chill for 2–3 hours or up to a day. Serve with plain saltine crackers.

Muffuletta Salsa with Salami Chips

FOR THE SALSA

1 (16-ounce) jar giardiniera
    pickled vegetables
1 (6-ounce) can pitted black
    olives
1 (6-ounce) can pitted green
    olives
1 (4-ounce) jar sliced
    pimentos
4 pepperoncini from a jar
2 tablespoons capers
1 clove garlic
2 tablespoons olive oil
1 tablespoon Italian herb
    seasoning
7 ounces provolone cheese

FOR THE SALAMI CHIPS

4 ounces thinly sliced
    Genoa salami, about
    1 inch in diameter

The muffuletta, along with po' boys, is part of the great New Orleans sandwich tradition. A symphony of olive and vegetable salad stacked high with cheese and cured meats layered between rounds of soft, chewy bread. You could make mini-muffulettas as a snack, but I love the change-up here, featuring a chunky version of the delicious olive salad scooped up with crisp salami chips.

SERVES 20

Rinse and drain the giardiniera, black and green olives, pimentos, and pepperoncini. Remove any stems from the pepperoncini. Place all the drained vegetables in the bowl of a food processor fitted with the steel blade. Add the capers with some of their liquid, the garlic, olive oil, and Italian seasoning. Pulse 5–8 times, stirring between pulses to get the larger pieces to the bottom, until you have a fine, loose relish. You do not want a paste but rather more of a rough salsa you can scoop up with the salami chips. Turn the salsa into a large bowl.

Finely dice the provolone and stir it into the salsa. I like to cut it into very small cubes, then run a large knife through the cubes several times as if chopping herbs. Do not be tempted to add the cheese to the food processor or grate it—it will make the salsa gummy.

Cover and refrigerate for at least 4 hours or up to 2 days.

To make the salami chips, preheat the oven to 375°. Line 2 rimmed baking sheets with parchment paper. Lay the salami slices in an even layer on the baking sheets. Bake the salami for 9–12 minutes, until the edges are slightly curled and beginning to brown. The chips will crisp further as they cool.

Notes: I ask the deli counter to cut a 7-ounce chunk of provolone rather than buying thin sandwich slices so that I can cut nice, square little cubes. I love the novel twist of serving this with salami chips, but I you could also dice some thick salami, as with the provolone, stir it into the salsa, and serve with baguette slices.

THE MARDI GRAS

I don't say things like this often, but I think every southerner should visit New Orleans during Mardi Gras season at least once in their life, to see the parade and the Second Lines. And every southerner should throw at least one Mardi Gras party. I went to a very small college in Connecticut, and in a precursor to my future life, I was in charge of the student activities committee my senior year. We threw cool parties, but I may have topped them all. I put on a Mardi Gras bash for my Yankee schoolmates complete with beads, doubloons, and a Zydeco band from New Orleans. I will admit, I don't remember much of the actual event—always the sign of a successful Mardi Gras—but it did get rave reviews. Mardi Gras is celebrated all over the South, with parades and full-on festivities throughout Louisiana and coastal Mississippi and Alabama, and with rocking parties in homes and bars everywhere else.

MARDI GRAS RECIPES
Calas with Charred Green Onion Dip
Petite Crawfish Pies
Shrimp with White and Red Remoulade
Cajun Popcorn (Fried Crawfish Tails)
Natchitoches Meat Pies with Buttermilk Dip
Grilled Andouille Doubloons with Sweet Potato Mustard
Muffuletta Salsa with Salami Chips

Nuts for Snacks

Sweet Tea Pecans

This nutty little nibble combines the best of the South: abundant pecans and our favorite refreshment. Sweet with a hint of salty finish, these nuts are a unique rendition of the classic treat. Make multiple batches—they will last in an airtight container for a week and freeze beautifully.

1 cup granulated sugar
2 cups water
3 black tea bags (such as orange pekoe)
12 ounces pecan halves
Kosher salt

MAKES 12 OUNCES

Stir the sugar and water together in a medium saucepan. Bring to a boil, reduce the temperature to medium and stir until the sugar is dissolved. Remove from the heat, drop in the teabags, and steep for 10 minutes. Remove the teabags and stir in the pecans. Soak for 45 minutes, stirring several times.

Heat the oven to 400°. Line a rimmed baking sheet with nonstick foil or parchment paper. Drain the pecans through a strainer, then spread in a single layer on the baking sheet. Sprinkle lightly with salt. Bake the pecans for 13–15 minutes, until golden brown. Watch carefully: nuts burn easily.

Cool the nuts on the baking sheet.

The nuts will keep in an airtight container for a week and can be frozen.

Bacon Pecan Saltine Toffee

1 pound bacon

About 50 saltine crackers

1 cup (2 sticks) unsalted
    butter

1 cup dark brown sugar

1 tablespoon bacon grease

1 tablespoon bourbon

1 cup finely chopped pecans

Flaky sea salt, such as
    Maldon (optional)

Cracker candy, as the non-bacon, chocolate-covered version of this is often called, has been a local favorite for years. I have made hundreds of batches in my time. When the sweet-salty bacon-in-dessert trend (bacon cupcakes! bacon donuts! bacon candy bars!) really started up, it occurred to me that adding salty bacon to the sweet toffee layer would make an interesting snack. And indeed it does—the combo is a great pairing for a cocktail or an icy glass of bourbon.

MAKES AT LEAST 100 PIECES

Cut the bacon into very small pieces and cook in a skillet over high heat until extra crispy and brown. Remove to paper towels to drain with a slotted spoon. Reserve 1 tablespoon of bacon grease.

Preheat the oven to 400°. Line a 12 × 18-inch rimmed baking sheet with nonstick foil or parchment paper. Lay the crackers out in a layer as close together as possible, filling the baking sheet.

Melt the butter, brown sugar, bacon grease, and bourbon in a medium saucepan over medium heat, stirring frequently. When the butter is melted, raise the heat to bring the mixture to a boil and boil for 3 minutes, stirring occasionally. After 3 minutes, give it a good stir and pour evenly over the crackers on the baking sheet. Spread the caramel around with a spatula if needed, but don't worry if the surface isn't covered completely—you just don't want it pooling in one place. Bake the crackers for 5 minutes, then remove from the oven and, working quickly, sprinkle the bacon pieces and pecans in an even layer over the crackers. Use a fork to break up any lumps and spread the topping evenly, lightly pressing the pieces into the toffee. The pieces need to adhere to the toffee, not layer on top of themselves. Sprinkle with sea salt, if using. Break the toffee into fragments and store in an airtight container for up to 5 days.

Barbecue Peanuts

We do a barbecue version of everything in Memphis. Nuts are no exception.

MAKES ABOUT 4 CUPS

Measure the spices together in a small jar and shake well to combine thoroughly.

Heat the oven to 375°. Spread the peanuts in an even layer on a rimmed baking sheet lined with parchment paper. Toast for 8–10 minutes, until they are wonderfully fragrant and golden.

Melt the butter in a large bowl. Add the toasted peanuts and sprinkle over 1 tablespoon of the spice mix. Stir well to coat the peanuts with the butter and the spice blend. Taste and add a little salt if you'd like. Spread the nuts back on the baking sheet and leave to cool. When the peanuts are completely cool, store them for up to a week in an airtight container.

1 tablespoon sweet paprika
½ teaspoons kosher salt
½ teaspoon celery salt
½ teaspoon freshly ground black pepper
¼ teaspoon onion powder
¼ teaspoon chili powder
¼ teaspoon crushed red pepper
¼ teaspoon garlic powder
¼ teaspoon smoked paprika
Pinch of cayenne pepper
16 ounces dry roasted peanuts
2 tablespoons (¼ stick) unsalted butter

UNCLE BILL'S PEANUTS

My aunt Joanne and uncle Bill lived in Hughes, Arkansas, when I was growing up. My brother and I would spend the weekend with them sometimes, undoubtedly to give my parents a much-needed break. Hughes was a small town, but it felt like out in the country to us. Aunt Jo and Uncle Bill had a trampoline in the backyard we could bounce on for hours. And we were endlessly fascinated by the shelves and shelves of trophies our older cousins had won playing football and as a majorette for big southern schools. But the treats I really remember are Uncle Bill's peanuts. He'd come home from the farm with a paper bag full of peanuts—I don't know where he got them—I don't think anyone around Hughes grew peanuts. He'd shell them, then toss them with butter and salt and roast them in the oven. Some kept their red papery skins; they fell off others. We'd eat the peanuts hot while my aunt worried that it would ruin our supper. No one else seems to remember these peanut treats, but they were the best peanuts I ever ate.

Boiled Peanuts

Boiled Peanuts are a love-or-hate thing. They are not crunchy like roasted peanuts, but soft and wet. Some people just can't get into the texture, as well as the fact that sometimes a little juice might squirt out when you open them up. Generally, you find someone selling boiled peanuts on the side of the road or at a country gas station. I myself had never considered boiling my own peanuts until I overheard a conversation about boiling them in the slow cooker. So I had to try. It works, it's easy, and it's a great treat when I find raw peanuts. Pull out a brown paper bag of goobers at a party, and a conversation about the merits or drawbacks is sure to ensue. I like my goobers with plenty of Creole seasoning and salt, but you could use just salt or any flavor combo you like.

I sometimes find raw peanuts, also called green peanuts, at farmers' markets but most often at Asian grocery stores. They are peanuts in the shell that have not been roasted.

1 pound raw peanuts

5 cups water

2 tablespoons Creole seasoning (such as Tony Chachere's)

2 tablespoons kosher salt

MAKES 1 POUND

Place the peanuts and the water in a slow cooker and stir in the seasonings. Cook on low for 10 hours, turn off the slow cooker, and leave the peanuts in the seasoned water for another 10–12 hours. Drain the peanuts and enjoy!

Boiled peanuts will keep covered for up to 3 days, but the drained peanuts can be frozen for up to 2 months. Reheat the peanuts in salted water to thaw.

Southern Goat Cheese with Boiled Peanut Relish

1 cup shelled boiled peanuts

3 green onions, white and
    light green parts

1 tablespoon parsley

Freshly ground black pepper

1 (8-ounce) log soft goat
    cheese

Should you have any leftover boiled peanuts, here is an elegant way to use them up. I often serve this pretty little dish alongside a big bowl of boiled peanuts, because once you have them, why not? Plus, there are so many southern dairies making wonderful goat cheese, I love to make the most of it.

MAKES ABOUT 1 CUP RELISH

Spread the shelled peanuts on a tea towel or paper towels and leave to air dry for about 30 minutes.

Roughly chop the peanuts a handful at a time and transfer to a small bowl. The peanuts are soft, so some will stick to your knife; just scrape them off and keep chopping. Finely chop the green onions and add to the bowl, then finely chop the parsley and add to the mix. Grind in some black pepper and gently stir to combine.

Cover the bowl and place in the refrigerator for a few hours to let the flavors blend.

Place the goat cheese on a platter and spoon the peanut relish over the top. Serve with simple crackers.

Benne Seed Wafer "Cocktailers"

Benne is an African word for sesame seed, where the seeds originate. Like okra and watermelon, the use of benne seeds in southern food is a direct result of the culinary knowledge of Africans caught in the slave trade. These benne wafers are the iconic snack of Charleston. A cookbook published in 1950 by the Junior League of Charleston, *Charleston Receipts*, is the oldest continuously published Junior League cookbook, and it undoubtedly relies on the recipes and traditions of African Americans who worked in private kitchens in the area. It is a good primer on Lowcountry cooking, so the perfect food souvenir of a visit to Charleston is a copy of *Charleston Receipts* and a tin of benne wafers. This is my slightly adapted version of the benne wafer recipe in that iconic cookbook. When the book was written, I doubt that tahini (sesame seed paste) was regularly available at the grocery, as it is now, and it adds a great little boost to the sesame richness.

1 cup white sesame seeds
2 cups all-purpose flour
1 teaspoon kosher salt
Dash of cayenne pepper
¾ cup vegetable shortening
1 teaspoon tahini (optional, but worth it)
¼–½ cup ice water
Kosher salt for sprinkling

MAKES ABOUT 36

Toast the sesame seeds in a dry skillet over medium heat until evenly golden brown. Use a spatula to keep the seeds moving around the pan, turning them so they cook evenly. When the seeds are golden, immediately spread on a plate to cool. Do not leave them in the pan or they will continue cooking and burn.

When the seeds are cooled, mix the flour, salt, and cayenne in the bowl of an electric mixer. Add the shortening, cut into small cubes, and the tahini, if using, and beat until the shortening is broken up and the mixture looks like damp sand. With the motor running, add the water a little at a time until the dough forms a ball. Add the benne seeds and beat until they are well mixed and evenly distributed. Knead the dough with your hands a few times to bring it all together.

At this point, you can roll the dough out on a lightly floured surface until ⅛ inch thick, then cut it into small rounds with a ½-inch biscuit cutter. Transfer the rounds to a baking sheet lined with parchment paper. Bake at 350° about 10–12 minutes, until lightly golden and firm. While the wafers are hot, sprinkle with salt, then move to a wire rack to cool completely.

Alternatively, you can roll 3 sections of the dough into narrow logs and wrap tightly in plastic wrap. Refrigerate the dough until firm, up to a week. When ready to cook, slice the logs into very thin wafers, place on a baking sheet lined with parchment paper and bake until lightly golden and firm, about 10–12 minutes. While the wafers are hot, sprinkle with salt, then move to a wire rack to cool completely.

THE SIP AND SEE

The sip and see is exactly as it sounds. An event where ladies drink and look at something. And it fits several occasions—when brides-elect (yes, that's what we used to call them) displayed their wedding presents and invited friends and family to come for tea and to exclaim upon the haul (and to make sure their gift was prominently and properly displayed). That tradition is not common now, but I have hosted and attended many a sip and see for a new baby. It is generally understood that a baby shower is hosted for the first child, before it is born, but a second child is given a sip and see, where it is presented in its finest embroidered clothing to be oohed and aahed over. Or grandmothers host a sip and see when their out-of-town grandchildren visit so all their friends can gaze in wonder upon their perfect progeny. A sip and see is a ladies' event, in the old-school style, china, silver, linens polished and pressed, flowers in a theme color, and delicate "lady" food. The sip is generally tea, most often iced because this is the South, but I count myself lucky that my experience with this event has always included wine.

SIP AND SEE RECIPES
Benedictine
Traditional Cheese Straws
Pecan Cheese Crisps
Cheese Crispies
Pepper Jelly Pimento Cheese
Crab Cake Bites with Artichoke Tartar Sauce
Shrimp Paste
Mustard Poppy Seed Ham Rolls
Asparagus with Lemon Chiffon Sauce
Sweet Tea Pecans

Nuts and Bolts

3 cups (6 sticks) unsalted butter
1 (2-ounce) bottle Tabasco sauce
1 cup Worcestershire sauce
1 (12-ounce) box corn Chex cereal
1 (14-ounce) box wheat Chex cereal
1 (9-ounce) bag oyster crackers
1 (16-ounce) bag pretzel sticks
1 (15.25-ounce) can deluxe mixed nuts (no peanuts)
1 (14-ounce) can roasted cashew halves and pieces

I suppose everyone has a recipe for this snack mix, but this one is based on my family's favorite version, and it is time-honored snack for my clan. My grandmother loved this, and in the waning years of her life, her lovely home helpers would make batches from the many handwritten recipe cards taped inside her kitchen cabinets. I make a batch every Christmas and give my brother a tin that is meant to be his own secret stash. I don't think he'd talk to me anymore if I stopped doing it. Package sizes have changed over the years, so I've had to adapt a little, but the essence is still there.

MAKES A HUGE AMOUNT

Melt the butter, Tabasco, and Worcestershire together in a saucepan.

Mix the cereals, crackers, and pretzel sticks together in a large, deep roasting pan or on 2 deep-rimmed baking sheets. I like to snap the pretzel sticks in half to make them easier to eat. Toss everything together with your hands, then pour over all but ½ cup of the melted butter and stir to coat everything well.

Preheat the oven to 200°. Cook the mix for 1 hour, then add the nuts and the remaining ½ cup butter and stir to combine. Continue cooking for a further 4 hours, stirring well about every 30–40 minutes. Cool completely.

The nuts and bolts can be kept in an airtight container for 2 weeks or can be frozen for 2 months. Thaw at room temperature before serving.

GAS STATION PEANUT BRITTLE

My mother is from Columbia, Tennessee, about an hour south of Nashville. When I was growing up, we used to drive to Columbia on weekends, leaving Friday after my dad got off work and returning home after church and Sunday lunch. Certain road treats made the long haul bearable for me and my brother: candy canes from a truck-stop diner, pecan rolls from Stuckey's, the occasional bag of chips and a soda, a restaurant called the Log Cabin where the waitress called you hon and the tea was way too sweet.

By the time I was old enough to drive to Columbia myself, a new highway was completed, and it cut the trip by about an hour but bypassed some of our old road haunts. The exit off the interstate to the shorter Minnie Pearl Parkway had one gas station. It was always clean and the people were very nice. No trip to Columbia was complete without a stop for gas and a restroom break (last chance for miles). But that little gas station's greatest redeeming feature was the homemade peanut brittle sold at the counter. It was the best peanut brittle I have ever had. Thick and full of peanuts, but not tooth-breakingly hard. Sweet and salty, but somehow almost creamy.

I started by picking up a bag each time I stopped in, then I started stocking up, bringing home pounds of the stuff to stash away. I wonder what that cashier thought of me buying six bags of brittle, a Diet Rite, and a tank of gas. Sadly, that station closed, but for the next few visits, I got off at the exit before to make use of the facilities and the brittle was for sale at that station for a while. Now that my grandparents have died, I don't make it to Columbia as often, but when I do go to see family that still live there, I stop in hopes of finding that brittle. But I never have.

Devils on Muleback (Pecan-Stuffed Dates Wrapped in Country Ham)

24 large Medjool dates

24 pecan halves

6 ounces country ham, sliced paper-thin

3 tablespoons pecan oil or olive oil

3 tablespoons apple cider vinegar

1 tablespoon honey

Many years ago, when I started entertaining in my first real home, my staple party appetizer was a recipe my aunt sent me, clipped out of a fancy cooking magazine. It was dates stuffed with a cube of Parmesan cheese, the whole wrapped in prosciutto and baked. It was easy to make, made fancy ingredients go a long way, and people absolutely devoured them. But it was published in a magazine with millions of readers, so eventually it became ubiquitous and I moved on to whatever became the next standard. Some community cookbooks have a recipe for devils on horseback featuring dates wrapped in bacon. But in thinking about wonderful snacks, it occurred to me that I could southern-ize this classic using native pecans and our own cured pork, country ham. I've added a vinaigrette to punch up the taste, and regionally pressed pecan oil adds an extra dimension of flavor. Look for country ham sliced as thinly as prosciutto.

MAKES 24

Slit the dates open without cutting all the way through. Remove the pits, press a pecan half into each date, and squeeze the date halves together. Cut the country ham into small pieces and wrap each date in the ham. Secure each wrapped date with a toothpick. The dates can be made up to 2 days ahead at this point, covered, and refrigerated.

When ready to serve, preheat the oven to 350°. Place the dates in a baking dish that just fits them—it's good to crowd them in. Put the oil, vinegar, and honey in a jar and shake to combine. Pour the vinaigrette evenly over the dates, then bake for 15 minutes. They will be very hot straight out of the oven, so let them cool a little before serving.

Pecan Biscuits with Ham and Bourbon Mayonnaise

FOR THE BISCUITS

4 cups soft wheat flour
(such as White Lily)

6 teaspoons baking powder

1½ teaspoons kosher salt

1 cup (2 sticks) unsalted
butter

1 cup finely chopped pecans

1 cup whole buttermilk

FOR THE MAYONNAISE

1 egg yolk, room
temperature

1 tablespoon fresh lemon
juice

1½ teaspoons Dijon
mustard

1 teaspoon freshly ground
black pepper

1 cup neutral oil (such as
vegetable, grapeseed,
or canola)

2 teaspoons bourbon

Kosher salt to taste

About ½ pound center-cut
country ham slices or
medium-thick sliced
smoked city ham

Ham biscuits are such a classic southern snack. Author Julia Reed even published a memoir titled *Ham Biscuits and Hostess Gowns.* There are many ways to make a ham biscuit, from a simple buttered biscuit stuffed with ham to overloaded cheese and ham butter-filled delights. But as you may have learned by now, I like to go the full southern. So I put pecans in the biscuits and bourbon in the mayonnaise, and I never skimp on the ham.

MAKES 25

For the biscuits, preheat the oven to 425°. Mix the flour, baking powder, and salt together in a large bowl using a fork. Cut the butter into small pieces and toss into the flour. Using your good clean hands or a pastry blender, rub the butter and flour together until you have a fine meal. Stir in the pecans until thoroughly combined. Add ¾ cup of the buttermilk and stir with a fork to combine. Now work the dough gently with your hands to form it into a cohesive mass. Add more buttermilk as needed. Lightly flour a surface and dump the dough onto it. Turn the dough over once or twice to bring it together, then roll out to ¼ inch thick with a lightly floured rolling pin. Cut into 2-inch squares or with a 2-inch round cutter dipped in flour. Place the biscuits very close together—almost touching—on 1 or 2 rimmed baking sheets lined with parchment paper. Bake for 8–10 minutes, until firm and lightly golden.

For the mayonnaise, place the egg yolk, lemon juice, Dijon, and black pepper in the bowl of a food processor. Blend to combine, then, with motor running, slowly drizzle in the oil in a slow, steady stream. Add the bourbon and a pinch of salt and pulse to combine. Scrape the mayonnaise into a bowl. Cover and refrigerate for several hours to firm up and allow the flavors to blend, but up to a day is fine.

To serve, cut the ham into biscuit-sized pieces, then split the biscuits in half and spread each side with a little mayonnaise. Add a sliver of ham and close each biscuit up.

Lagniappe

Cream Cheese Wafer Biscuits

1 cup (2 sticks) unsalted
butter, softened
8 ounces cream cheese,
softened
2 cups all-purpose flour
1 teaspoon kosher salt

I have stumbled across versions of this recipe in many community cookbooks over the years, and after seeing it so many times, I just had to try it to see if it's for real. The recipe is so easy, I suspected it was too good to be true. But, lo and behold, it works.

I have seen it titled cream cheese biscuits and cream cheese wafers, but neither is completely accurate. These are really a combination of the two. It's a little difficult to describe: they're crumbly and soft but develop a crispy outside. The cream cheese adds tang, and the butter brings richness. The lazy lady's food-processor method is my own twist, and it makes this simple recipe even quicker. These little gems are an interesting vehicle for a hearty spread or served topped with a little ham or bacon.

MAKES ABOUT 24

Cut the butter and the cream cheese into chunks and drop into the bowl of a food processor fitted with the metal blade. Process for a few seconds to combine. Add the flour and the salt, and process until the dough forms a ball. Divide the dough in half and plop each piece onto a piece of waxed paper. Form into logs about 2 inches in diameter, and roll tightly in the paper, twisting the ends like candy wrappers. Refrigerate until firm, for a least 2 hours, but up to 2 days is fine.

When ready to bake, preheat the oven to 350°. Line a baking sheet with parchment paper. Slice the dough rolls into biscuits about ½ inch thick and place on the baking sheet. Bake until firm and lightly golden on the edges, about 10–12 minutes. Cool before serving.

Cornbread Thins

Spread thin onto a baking sheet, cornbread cooks up firm and perfect for supporting a host of things. Try these with Creamy Collard Dip (page 6) spooned on top or instead of biscuits with the country ham and bourbon mayonnaise (page 152).

MAKES 24 (2-INCH) SQUARES

1 cup stone-ground yellow cornmeal
1 cup all-purpose flour
¼ cup granulated sugar
4 teaspoons baking powder
½ teaspoon kosher salt
1 large egg
1 cup whole buttermilk
¼ cup vegetable oil

Preheat the oven to 400°. Line a 15½ × 10½-inch rimmed baking sheet with nonstick foil or parchment paper, with some hanging over the edges to make it easy to lift out when cooked.

Mix the cornmeal, flour, sugar, baking soda, and salt together well in a large bowl. Add the egg, buttermilk, and oil and stir until thoroughly combined, with no dry ingredients visible in the bowl. Scrape the batter into the prepared pan, then use an offset spatula to spread the batter evenly in the pan. It will be thin, but make sure there are no gaps with the pan showing through.

Bake the cornbread for 15 minutes, until the top is evenly golden brown and dry. Cool completely in the pan, then lift out the foil lining and cut the cornbread into squares or strips.

LAGNIAPPE

Lagniappe is a delightful term with roots in French and Spanish Louisiana that means "a little something extra." Mark Twain described it as "a word worth traveling to New Orleans to get; a nice limber, expressive, handy word."

Bacon Crackers

4 strips of bacon

1¾ cups all-purpose flour

1½ teaspoons baking
powder

¼ teaspoon kosher salt,
plus more for sprinkling

1 tablespoon solidified
bacon grease

5 tablespoons unsalted
butter, cold, cut into
small cubes

½–⅔ cup very cold water

1 tablespoon butter, melted

Making homemade crackers is one of the little culinary secrets I love so much. It never occurs to most people that making your own is something that can be done. But it is easy to do and pretty impressive when you serve homemade crackers. These crispy, salty squares take pimento cheese spread to a whole new level. These are excellent on any cheese platter, with a creamy brie, a salty chèvre, or a tangy blue. Or smeared with a little butter. Frankly, they are good all on their own.

If you have a fancy-edged pastry roller, this is a great place to use it. Personally, I like the rough and rustic look. Not all my crackers are even or perfect, but if I actually make my own crackers, I want them to look homemade! The crackers do need to be roughly the same size on the same baking sheet for even cooking.

MAKES ABOUT 36

Preheat the oven to 350°. Line 2 rimmed baking sheets with silicone liners or parchment paper.

Cook the bacon in a skillet until very crispy. Remove to paper towels to drain with a slotted spoon.

Pat the cooled bacon with paper towels to remove as much grease as possible. Break the bacon into pieces into the bowl of a food processor fitted with the steel blade. Pulse several times to chop the bacon very finely. Scrape the bacon out of the bowl and set aside. Do not worry if some bacon residue remains on the sides of the bowl.

Place the flour, baking soda, salt, and 1 tablespoon of the chopped bacon in the food processor and pulse a few times to combine. Add the bacon grease and the butter pieces. Pulse several times until the mixture looks like sand, with a few larger lumps throughout. Turn on the food processor and drizzle in the ice-cold water until the dough starts to come together. Check the dough by pinching a bit between your fingers. If it sticks together, you're done. You may use slightly less water, but you may need a touch more. Add another tablespoon of chopped bacon bits and pulse a few times to mix them through the dough. You may have a little extra bacon. Lucky you.

Lightly flour a work surface. Divide the cracker dough in half and place one piece on the work surface. Knead it a little to bring the dough together and pat it into a square. Using a floured rolling pin, roll the dough until it is as thin as a dime, trying your best to keep it in an even rectangle. Trim off the rough edges and set aside (see Note). Cut the dough into crackers, about 1 × 1 inch. I find a pizza wheel to be a very handy tool for this. You can cut the dough into smaller crackers if you prefer, but you'll need to adjust the cooking time. Carefully transfer the crackers to the prepared baking sheets. The crackers puff up rather than out, so you can place them close together. Prick the top of the crackers with a fork, then very lightly brush the tops with melted butter and lightly sprinkle with salt. Repeat with the second half of the dough. Bake the crackers, a sheet at a time, in the middle of the oven for 12–15 minutes, until lightly puffed, golden brown, and firm. Cool on the baking sheets.

The crackers will keep in a completely airtight container for several days. I find that a flat, sturdy container works best; a zippered bag doesn't protect the crackers from breakage very well.

Note: I like to gather all the scraps and knead them together, then roll them out as sort of a third batch. They may be not as pretty as the rest, but they taste just as good.

Cocktail Biscuits

2 cups soft wheat flour
(such as White Lily)
3 teaspoons baking powder
¾ teaspoons kosher salt
½ cup (1 stick) unsalted
butter
1 cup whole buttermilk

Everything is better with biscuits, our favorite snacks included. Little biscuits are perfect to serve with beef tenderloin, pork tenderloin, country ham, city ham . . . do I really need to go on?

MAKES ABOUT 25

Preheat the oven to 450°. Mix the flour, baking powder, and salt together in a large bowl using a fork. Cut the butter into small pieces and toss into the flour. Using your good clean hands or a pastry blender, rub the butter and flour together until you have a fine meal. Add ¾ cup of the buttermilk and stir with a fork to combine. Now work the dough gently with your hands to bring it together in a nice cohesive mass. Add more buttermilk as needed. Lightly flour a surface and dump the dough onto it. Turn the dough over once or twice to bring it together, then roll out to ¼ inch thick with a lightly floured rolling pin. Cut into 2-inch squares or with a 2-inch round cutter dipped in flour. Place the biscuits very close together—almost touching—on 1 or 2 rimmed baking sheets lined with parchment paper. Bake for 8–10 minutes, until firm and lightly golden.

Firecrackers

We all have deep and personal food memories and cravings. Exotic postcard moments in our life in food. Apricots still warm from the tree in France. The first taste of fish cooked immediately after being pulled from the Indian Ocean. Or cravings that seem to come deep from the soul and out of the clear blue sky. The special multilayered cake only your grandmother knew how to make. Bread from the long-ago-shuttered, family-owned neighborhood bakery. Your mom's homemade soup. This recipe is none of those things. It is not exotic or distant or impossible to duplicate. But it is a good food memory for me and, I bet, for a lot of folks. I just know how to make these. I didn't invent them or innovate them or deconstruct or reimagine. These little crackers are just good and simple, and everyone loves them. Though I make a habit of staying away from packaged mixes, I make an exception for these spicy gems. I use mild chili powder and a small amount of chili flakes, but feel free to spice things up.

1½ cups vegetable oil
1 (1-ounce) package ranch dip mix
1 tablespoon chili powder
2 teaspoons crushed red chili flakes
1 (16-ounce) box saltine crackers

MAKES ABOUT 120

In a small bowl, whisk together the canola oil, ranch dip mix, chili powder, and pepper flakes until thoroughly combined. Unwrap the saltines and place in 2 1-gallon zip-top bags or a large, shallow airtight container, such as you might store brownies in. Pour over the oil and toss and shake well to coat. Give the bags or container a toss every 5 minutes or so for about an hour, making sure the crackers are getting a thorough dose of seasoned oil.

Remove the crackers to 1 or 2 rimmed baking sheets and leave to dry for several hours. Stored in an airtight container, these will last for a couple of weeks. But I bet they don't.

SOUTHERN CHEESES

Belle Chèvre, bellechevre.com

Blackberry Farm, blackberryfarm.com/shop

iGourmet, igourmet.com

Looking Glass Creamery, ashevillecheese.com

Sweet Grass Dairy, sweetgrassdairy.com

COUNTRY HAM, SAUSAGE, AND CHARCUTERIE

Benton's Smoky Mountain Country Hams (country ham and
the world-famous smoked bacon), bentonscountryham.com

Blackberry Farm (charcuterie), blackberryfarm.com/shop

Cajun Grocer (boudin, andouille, crawfish tails), cajungrocer
.com

Edwards Virginia Hams (country ham, thin-sliced Surryano
ham), edwardsvaham.com

Newsoms Country Hams (ground country ham), newsoms
countryham.com

Olli Salumeria (charcuterie), olli.com

SOUTHERN PANTRY

Anson Mills (stone-ground grits, benne seeds, heirloom grain
flours), ansonmills.com

Batch (hot sauce, honey, seasonings), batchusa.com

Bourbon Barrel Foods (bourbon-barrel-aged soy sauce,
Worcestershire sauce, and bourbon-barrel-smoked paprika)
bourbonbarrelfoods.com

Braswell's (pepper jelly), braswells.com

Cajun Grocer (hot sauce, Creole seasoning), cajungrocer.com

Critchfield Meat Market (beaten biscuits), critchfieldmeats.com

Low Country Produce (pickles and relishes), lowcountry
produce.com

Oliver Farms (pecan oil, pecan flour, green peanut oil),
oliverfarm.com

SOURCES FOR INGREDIENTS

Perre Coleman Magness is the author of *Pimento Cheese: The Cookbook: 50 Recipes from Snacks to Main Dishes Inspired by the Classic Southern Favorite*, and *The Southern Sympathy Cookbook: Funeral Food with a Twist*. She is also the cook behind the website The Runaway Spoon, which focuses on creative recipes with a definite southern slant. Her work also appears in *Edible Memphis, OKRA: The Magazine of the Southern Food and Beverage Museum*, and the *Christian Science Monitor Online*.

Perre has studied food and cooking around the world, mostly by eating, but also through serious study. Coursework at Le Cordon Bleu London and intensive courses in Morocco and Thailand as well as seminars in Mexico, Santa Fe, and Memphis have broadened her culinary skill and palate. But her kitchen of choice is at home, cooking like most people, experimenting with unique but practical ideas.

College in Connecticut and graduate school in England taught her to cherish her southern roots, to learn and explore all the flavors that make the South so special. Perre has traveled extensively, from Egypt to Zimbabwe, India to South Africa, Peru to Indonesia, Burma to Spain, Tunisia to Cambodia, and just keeps going. She could relate at least two meals at each destination as her primary memories of each journey.

Mustard Poppy Seed Ham
    Rolls, 112
Natchitoches Meat Pies with
    Buttermilk Dip, 90–93, 92
Sweet and Spicy Pecan Pepper
    Cocktail Bacon, 96–97
Sweet Tea–Brined Pork Tender-
    loin with Sweet Tea Mustard,
    88, 89
Venison Bruschetta with
    Cumberland Gap Sauce,
    107
meatballs, 94–95
meat pies, 90–93, 92
Memphis, Tenn., 19, 49, 98, 99,
    139
midnight snacks, 86
mignonette, 76, 77
mini-muffins, 128
Mississippi, 48, 50, 56, 57, 94, 110,
    117, 120, 121
Mississippi Sin, 4, 5, 13
Muffuletta Salsa with Salami
    Chips, 132, 133, 134
Mule Day, 110
mustard
    Andouille Doubloons with
        Sweet Potato Mustard, 87
    Catfish Bites with Beer Sauce,
        57
    Country Ham Paté, 26
    Deviled Egg Spread, 24
    Jezebel Jelly, 44
    Mustard Poppy Seed Ham
        Rolls, 112
    Shrimp with White and Red
        Remoulade, 70–71
    Sweet Tea–Brined Pork Tender-
        loin with Sweet Tea Mustard,
        88, 89
Mustard Poppy Seed Ham Rolls,
    112, 147

N
nachos, barbecue, 98
Natchitoches Meat Pies with
    Buttermilk Dip, 90–93, 92,
    134
New Orleans, La.
    about, 134
    recipes from, 60, 61–62, 132,
        133, 134
nuts, 135–52
    Bacon Pecan Saltine Toffee, 138
    Barbecue Peanuts, 139
    Benne Seed Wafer "Cocktail-
        ers," 144, 145–46
    Boiled Peanuts, 140, 141
    Devils on Muleback (Pecan-
        Stuffed Dates Wrapped in
        Country Ham), 150, 151
    Nuts and Bolts, 148
    Pecan Biscuits with Ham and
        Bourbon Mayonnaise, 152
    Southern Goat Cheese with
        Boiled Peanut Relish, 142, 143
    Sweet Tea Pecans, 136, 137
Nuts and Bolts, 13, 148

O
okra, 51
onions, 19, 22–23, 131
    See also green onions
opening day of dove season
    recipes, 106
Overnight Onions, 13, 131
oysters, 76, 77

P
pancakes, 124, 125
parties and recipe lists
    Derby Day, 40
    Mardi Gras, 134
    opening day of dove season,
        106

sip and see, 147
tailgating, 13
Party Tomato Pies, 114, 115–16
pâté, 26, 73
peanut brittle, 149
peanuts, 139, 140, 141, 142, 143, 149
Pecan Biscuits with Ham and
    Bourbon Mayonnaise, 40, 152
Pecan Cheese Crisps, 31, 147
Pecan Pepper Cocktail Bacon, 13,
    96–97
pecans
    Bacon Pecan Cheese Ball, 41
    Bacon Pecan Saltine Toffee, 138
    Classic Cheese Ring with
        Strawberry Preserves, 39–40
    Country Ham Cheesecake,
        42, 43
    Devils on Muleback (Pecan-
        Stuffed Dates Wrapped in
        Country Ham), 150, 151
    Hot Pecan Country Ham
        Spread, 25
    Pecan Biscuits with Ham and
        Bourbon Mayonnaise, 152
    Pecan Cheese Crisps, 31
    Pepper Jelly, 45
    Sweet and Spicy Pecan Pepper
        Cocktail Bacon, 96–97
    Sweet Tea Pecans, 136, 137
Pecan-Stuffed Dates Wrapped in
    Country Ham. See Devils on
    Muleback
pepper jelly, 36, 37, 38, 42, 45
Pepper Jelly Pimento Cheese, 38,
    147
Persimmon Chutney, 108–9
Petite Crawfish Pies, 78–79, 134
Pickapeppa Sauce, 45
pickled green beans, 126, 127
pickled shrimp, 68, 69
pickled watermelon rind, 76, 77

·